WAS IT LIKE THIS FOR YOU?

First published in 1995 by
Woodfield Publishing

A catalogue record of this book
is available from the British Library

ISBN 1 873203 31 4

Printed and bound in Great Britain

Was it Like This For You?

A collection of humorous reminiscences
of the Royal Air Force in peace and war.

Contributed by members of
No. 310 Branch, Royal Air Forces Association,
Leamington Spa, Warwick & District

Woodfield

№ 310

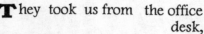
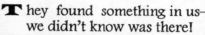
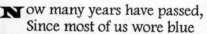

No. 310 Branch, Royal Air Forces Association, Leamington Spa, Warwick & District

Contents

Illustrations

Foreword

At the end of the First World War, a number of Squadron and Unit associations were formed to enable those who had served together to maintain contact with one another. It was not, however, until 1930 that an organisation known as the Comrades of the Royal Air Force was formed, with the membership irrespective of rank, to those serving or who had served in the Royal Air Force, the Royal Flying Corps, Royal Naval Air Service and Dominion Air Forces. Marshal of the Royal Air Force, Lord Trenchard was the first President.

The women who had served with the Royal Air Force in WW1 had, in 1919, formed an old comrades association to which were admitted members of the Women's Auxiliary Air Force. Both organisation had worked in close co-operation and after the outbreak of the Second World War in 1939 agreed to amalgamate.

In 1943 the name was changed to the present title of the Royal Air Forces Association, with membership available to all who are serving or who have served in the Royal Air Forces of the Crown, and the Association received official recognition by the Air Ministry. Branches were grouped into regions, Councils were formed on which regions were represented and, most importantly, the welfare services were instituted, covering legal and general advice on pensions and employment.

The Royal Leamington Spa, Warwick & District Branch is one of the largest branches outside the cities of the Midlands, and as such the branch welfare officer is much in demand. Any member or ex-member of the Flying Services is assured a welcome. There is a regular programme of social activities which caters for all tastes.

Welfare subjects are always at the forefront of members minds as we are committed to look after not just our own branch members but also those who have served their time, their widows and their dependants.

All the contributors to this book have very kindly given their services free for which we thank them. A very big thank you must go to Derek Waters for the original idea for the book and also for most of the stories and cartoons.

Mike Harrison
Secretary, 310 Branch RAFA

The Contributors

The ex-RAF personnel who have provided their reminiscences to this book served in a wide range of ranks, trades and categories and are representative of the membership of any RAFA, or RAF formation today.

They are:-

Sid Arscott • Frank Beasley • Doug Castle • John Dawe

Bernard Dee • John Drew • John Edwards

Mike Harrison • John Heath • Hugh Oxley

Gordon Powis • Roy Rowberry • Reg Sharp

Bob Stow • R. Suppards • Alan Turner

Arthur Walton • Derek Waters

Plus an anonymous ex-Flt.Lt. Canberra pilot.

Many RAF people, past and present, went through pre-service training in the Air Training Corps, and when their active service days were ended they returned to help train other young men for the flying services. As Wing Commander John Dawe (RAFVRT) shows in his contribution, this association is still alive and well.

Introduction

The stories in this book have been gathered from several sources. Some are reprints from the monthly Newsletter of 310 Branch, others are reminiscences from "volunteer" members too slow to get away from the Secretary, Mike Harrison, who also provided some stories of his own (long-ago!) youth.

Many of the airfields, training bases and radar stations mentioned in the following pages, which once hummed with the activities of war and the uneasy peace which followed, have long since been declared redundant, and have disappeared to make way for building land and motorways. As for the aircraft... there are a few left languishing in museums, but the vast majority went to the scrap-yards many years ago.

But, as far as the people who contributed to this little book are concerned, in their memories those airfields, the friends they made, the incidents they write of are as fresh in their minds as if they happened yesterday.

All the stories following are humorous as we hope the readers will agree, and indeed in some cases the title could have been "Now It Can Be Told", because some of the respectable inhabitants of the area covered by 310 Branch have revealed incidents in their past which show that they were not always such solid, law-abiding citizens as they appear today!

The "links" and some of the stories were written by R. Suppards (who spent his formative years in a state of considerable confusion as his name implies); the cartoons are by Derek Waters (who can't draw but tries hard) and the editors are Derek Waters and Mike Harrison.

A MESSAGE FROM THE EDITORS FOLLOWS:

'PLEASE BUY OUR BOOK!'

All authors royalties go to the Royal Air Forces Association, 310 Branch.

Recruit Daze

"YOU 'ORRIBLE LITTLE MAN... WOT ARE YOU?"

"'OO TOLD YOU TO FALL OVER ON PARADE?"

"AND WHAT WERE YOU BEFORE YOU JOINED THE SERVICE, PLONK?" ... "HAPPY, SIR!"

"SUGAR... ONE DIP OR TWO?"

WAS IT LIKE THIS FOR YOU?

CHAPTER I

The Beginning

To all of us life in the RAF began with the receipt of a little buff envelope sent to us on the service of His Majesty enclosing a Railway Warrant inviting us to travel Third Class to be at the Royal Air Force Station nominated at a certain date, and before a specified time.

Often the recruit was invited not only to find the place – but report to the 'Attestation Waiting Room.'

But what (and where) *was* the Attestation Waiting Room? Of course it was actually where you went to be "attested" (i.e. "sworn in"), but every night at Warrington Banque (pronounced *bang-key*) Railway Station, where most airmen-to-be arrived on their way to Padgate, the SPs carried out a sweep search for those who, devoid of hope, had mistakenly chosen to report to the *station* waiting room!".

Having sworn to do our duty "unto death", for most of us realisation did not strike fully home until we were marched to Main Stores to draw our kit. To those of us who grew up in wartime Britain, where clothes rationing allowed only one suit a year, the list seemed endless. Remember?

KIT LIST		
Cap Badge	Boots (Best) 1pr	Ration Bag
F/s.Cap	Socks (Wool) 3pr	Waterbottle
Tunics 2	Housewife	Waterbottle cover
Slacks .... 2pr.	Mess Tin	Brushes.................... 4
Greatcoat	Mess Tin Strap........ 1	Black tie 2
Vests 2	Webbing Belt	Button Stick
Underpants 2pr	Cross Straps 2	Shirts 3
P.T. Vests 2	L Straps 2	Collars 6
P.T. Shorts 2pr	Bayonet Frog	Collar Studs 1pr
P.T. Slippers 1pr	Kit-bag	
Groundsheet	Big Pack	*Plus a deficiency chit*
Boots, A.P. 1pr	Small Pack	*for unissued items*

And, of course, everything needed either scrubbing or blanco-ing, polishing or pressing, darning or laundering. Some Mums were happy that the apple of their eye was learning the skills that would make him a good wife one day – others received a parcel of dirty washing and holey socks to darn each week!

The pay could hardly have been called generous, it was 28/- per week, paid fortnightly in arrears, less stoppages (for things like barrack damages) and credits. Also the Air Force pointed out that within the sum of 4/- per day (before stoppages) was a provision for "Airmen's Necessaries" – not, as you might think, fags and beer, but Blanco, Duraglit, Soldiers Friend, Shaving Soap, Ordinary Soap, darning wools, cotton, razor blades and collar studs which were *ALWAYS* breaking.

All these "Necessaries" were sold in the NAAFI. Since, as a recruit you were not allowed off Camp for the first six weeks, the NAAFI did a roaring trade. The NAAFI remitted part of its profit back to the Air Force. It was no wonder with two such powerful organizations conspiring to part the airman from his pay that there was always too much fortnight left at the end of the pay! But in those first six weeks, poverty was the least of our worries.

There was a credit side though: we knew our rank, Aircraftsman Second Class (AC2); our trade, Aircrafthand General Duties (ACH/GD), which was the lowest of the low in the Air Force hierarchy, and there was a certain comfort to be gained from knowing that you could sink no lower. Also we knew our Service number, our 1250 number, and our rifle number.

Also, like Pavlov's dogs we learned to respond immediately to certain stimuli. For example, if a voice in harsh and vulgar tone shouted, "Oi, you, airman!", you stopped what you were doing, came to attention and shouted your name and 'last three'. There were times when you half believed it was your parents who'd christened you "Jones 498".

And the names you got called! I remember feeling distinctly aggrieved when told that I was "standing there like a pregnant earwig", but I soon felt a fit of the giggles coming on when another fellow was told that he was the sort that "only a mother could love"!

Padgate, February 1947 – Highland Courtesy

We were in our second week on the Flights, square-bashing. At the opposite end of the hut from me there was a gigantic Scot who came from a place in the Northern fastnesses called Rumbling Bridge. Like many really big lads there was not an ounce of vice in him, and his main characteristic was a simple gentleness.

Each week his "Maw" sent him the Scottish Sunday papers. In the evening he would lie on his pit and chuckle at the exploits of "Oor Wullie and the Broons." He made the rest of us Southern cynics smile at his laughter.

Yet he was the first erk in our hut to be put on a charge. It happened this way. One night he set off to go to No. 2 Wing NAAFI, got lost in the darkness,

More Recruit Daze

"TAKE YER 'AT ORF LADDIE... THERE AIN'T NO WOODPECKERS IN 'ERE!"

REGIMENT CORPORAL: "NAH, THIS AFTERNOON YOU 'AVE LEARNT 'OW TO KILL A MAN WIV YER DINNER SPOON!"

"FLAK ALLEY!"

and in error stumbled into the Recruits NAAFI which was strictly *verboten* to those already square-bashing.

As he came in out of the darkness the Canteen Corporal, a little Cockney cock-sparrow of a man, half Jock's size came up to him and yapped, "Who are you?" To which Jock looked down pleasantly on the Corporal and warmly replied, "Aahm fine mon, and Hoos yersel'?"

Luckily our Flight Commander was a kindly man, and Jock was only admonished, but the two erks from our hut who had furnished the "Prisoner's Escort" were the ones who needed sympathy as they were given a right "reprimanding" for laughing.

The Flight Commander had asked Jock why he'd not replied to the Corporal's question with his name, rank and last three. To which Jock answered, "Well sir, when he asked me the question, I thocht the wee mannie was just being polite, I didna' realise at the time that it was a chargeable offence to be polite to a Corporal!"

R. Suppards

2360082 TOBINS D.

Don Tobins was a Peterborough lad who was in the next bed to me at Padgate. We were Square-bashing. He was a good oppo but quite an unremarkable bloke until the occasion when he had the whole Flight crying with laughter.

We started square-bashing on Feb. 3rd 1947. It was a terrible winter. The worn-out railway stock couldn't cope with the weather, the Miners were on strike, the roads were impassable and Padgate was to all intents and purposes cut off from the outside world. This situation was to go on until early April. There was no coke for the training flights, what little there was reserved for the Hospital, which was full of cases, many suffering from Meningitis. Food was down to three tins of M&V per day. Whole huts disappeared into the stoves in the Training Wings – but still the training went on.

Came the day when we were sent over the snow covered Assault Course. Part of the course led over a stream about fifteen feet wide, which naturally enough was ice-covered. To cross it you had to run over a steel tube about a foot in diameter.

Clutching my rifle I got across by running so fast, my feet barely touched the tube (studded AP boots with snow on them gave a very poor grip!). Don followed me. First his left foot slipped on the tube, and with superhuman gyrations he recovered his balance. Gingerly he took his next step. Then the Corporal DI shouted, "Come on lad, get your finger out , and MOVE!!"

That finished it for Don, he took a hesitant half step, then slowly, almost wearily, slipped head-first into the stream through the ice! His Chaplinesque

Still More Recruit Daze

ballet had got most people laughing, but there was a moment's concern as those who had crossed, and those waiting to cross waited for him to surface again.

Spluttering, Don stood up (the water was only about five feet deep), waded to the bank and stood dripping in front of the Corporal who was beside himself. "Where's your gun?" he howled.

Don seemed partly stunned, he looked carefully at his left hand... no rifle there, then he inspected his right... no rifle there either. He looked blankly at the Corporal.

Even I, his friend, sorry for him as I was, could not resist a snigger. The rest of the Flight were openly laughing at this display.

"Go back and get it!" yelled the Corporal.

Don turned on his heel, and like a robot strode down the bank to the spot where he'd fallen in, bent down until he was completely submerged, and dredged up his rifle. He then opened the bolt and sloshed the rifle around underwater, then lifted the rifle so that the water in the breech ran out of the barrel.

"You bloody fool !" yelled the Corporal, "you'll make it rusty! Get out of the water!"

We could see that Don was suffering dreadfully with the effects of the cold, but what with the duckweed clinging to his denims and his antics there wasn't a dry eye in the Flight!

The Corporal took off his battledress blouse and put it over Don's shoulders and ordered us to double back to the hut lines. That night the two stoves in our hut glowed red hot as we burned the partitions between the latrines to try to get Don warm again.

The following morning we were issued with Railway Warrants, 295s and Ration Cards and sent home. It was six weeks before we were called back. Don said that all the time he was at Padgate complete strangers would come up to him and ask, "Have you cleaned your rifle lately?" and then walk away sniggering.

R. Suppards.

BONFIRE NIGHT

This sprog was commanded to RAF Padgate on 5th November 1952 and upon arrival was allocated together with another twenty or so lost souls to the usual wooden hut, heated by the usual coke stove.

It was 'suggested' by the NCO who had been lumbered with this motley crew, that we should get the fire going, so being eager to do something rather than nothing in these unfamiliar surroundings, and being anxious to find as

WAS IT LIKE THIS FOR YOU?

much comfort as possible in the circumstances, I started to stuff paper, wood etc. into the menacing-looking black cylindrical monster and put a match to it.

"Right, fall in outside, stop what you are doing, over to the mess," (for our first RAF meal) ordered the NCO.

Upon return to the hut, we were a little surprised to find an NCO, a puddle and the Orderly Officer poking at the charred floorboards round the edge of a hole, just in front of "my" stove.

Neither the NCO nor the OO were at all appreciative of my efforts to warm up the hut (as ordered) and were most critical of my intelligence, and my parentage. I felt it inappropriate to remind them that "after all it was BONFIRE NIGHT!"

Alan Turner

A FRIENDLY GREETING

On arrival at the "resort" of RAF Hednesford up on Cannock Chase for two months's square-bashing late in November 1952 aboard "luxury coaches" provided by the tour company (actually five-ton trucks with canvas tops and wooden benches down the sides which had picked us up from the local main-line railway station), we were welcomed by a snow flurry, a foretaste of things to come ("No high ground in that direction between here and the Ural mountains, mate!") and by a tall, erect individual with a well-worn, and well shrunk beret who invited us to disembark into the snow flurry.

"RIGHT YOU LOT! OUTSIDE ON THE ROAD IN YER P.T. KIT IN FIVE MINUTES! COME ON MOVE!!"

DW.

ERK'S VOCABULARY

In addition to everything else there was a new set of words to learn. Here are just a few of them:

Ackers. Cash – A very scarce commodity.

Bird. Female.
Bint. Female (Arabic).
Bundook. Rifle (Hindi).
Blood-wagon. Ambulance.
Bull Night. Domestic clean-up night.
Bind. To rail against the inevitable.
Burton. To go for this was usually fatal.
Blower. Telephone. Often answered as, "Guardroom here!" (speaking offices were commonplace).
Brat. Apprentice. Devotee to ACIs and the Manual of Air Force Law.
Boots, AP. Army Pattern/Armour Piercing (stopping distance 100 yards).
Brown-Types. Army personnel.
Blue Types. Naval Personnel.
Blues. These could be Best, or Working uniforms.
Belt Up! Shut up! Interchangeable with Wrap up!
Brassed off. Generally displeased. Also 'browned off', 'cheesed off' or 'chokker'.
"Back in the dark days". Common "old hands" preamble to a story (Often followed by, "When it was rough").

Clot. Nincompoop.
Chop. Going for this was fatal.
Chop Board. Appearing before this could damage your prospects.
Chiefy. F/Sgt. Calling them this was *NOT* well received.
Cha/Chi. Airman's drink – was it laced with bromide?
Charp/Charpoy. (Hindi) Bed – also 'kip' or 'pit'.
Chokker. (see 'brassed off') Airman's normal state of mind.

Docs. Airman's Record. Nearly always 'lost' in Pay Accounts (resulting in perpetual underpayment).
Dim. Dim as a NAAFI candle (not very bright).
Deficiency Chit. List of un-issued kit.
Doofer. Fag end, usually kept behind left ear (*do for* now/later)
D.I. Drill Instructor. One was known as Old Mouth-in-Trousers (perhaps they all were.)

Erk. Aircraftsman.
Eating Irons. Airman's Cutlery. Also, *in extremis* replaced side-arms, *vide* Ground Combat Instructors.

Form 252. Charge Form. Being on one was a great cause of being chokker.
Form 295. Leave Form. Often issued with travel warrant and Ration Card.
Form 700. Aircraft Serviceability record. You always had a twinge when you signed one.
Finger Trouble. Inefficiency. Sometimes used in the phrase "you've got your finger in your ear (or other orifice) and your mind in neutral!"
F.F.I. Short-arm Inspection. Often myths were exposed as just that! Myths!
F.L. Windsock. So called because of its resemblance to one. (origin: pharmaceutical.)
Flap. Running around in small circles waving the arms in the air and squeaking.
Flight Louey. A Flight Lieutenant (in fact any Flight Lieutenant!)

Golden Eagle Day. Pay Parade.
George. Auto-pilot (a great improvement on real ones!).
Groupie. Affectionate (?) term for a Group Captain.
Gremlin. Evil or mischievous gnome.
Glasshouse. Corrective Establishment.

Huff Duff. H/F.
Hairy. A frightening experience. Often described as "not very hairy – in fact hardly hairy at all!" (false modesty!).
Hanger Doors. "Close them!" meant stop talking shop.

IFF. Radar Identification Friend or Foe – a sort of electronic FFI.

Jankers. Defaulters Punishment.

Kifer. (Arabic) Very impolite form of Bint.
Keen Type. A severe pain in the neck.

Line. A story which is/or may be far-fetched. Often accompanied by lamp-swinging.

M.I. Room. Sick Bay (normally only prescribed M&D).

Mucker. Pal (put you to bed when drunk and lent you money).

Matelot. Sailor (what were those stories about the Golden Rivet?)

Nig-Nog. No racial connotation – it just meant dimmer than dim.

Orderly Room. Staffed by power-mad maniacs. Aided and abetted Pay A/cs and Records Gloucester in losing Airman's Docs and posting people to the wrong stations via impossible routes.

'Orrible Little Man. Criticism often levelled at erks by angry Corporals.

Oppo. Opposite number (see Mucker).

Plumbers. Engineering Wing. Believed to subscribe to the axiom "If you can't fix it f--- it!"

Passion-Killers. WAAF Underwear.

Pig-Sticker. Short bayonet.

Prang. Originally crash, also used as a description for a successful attack.

Pongo. Soldier (common airman's belief that they had all been dropped on their heads as babies.)

Pit. See Charp.

Put up a black. More serious form of dropping a clanger.

Pot/Pialah. The latter is of Malayan origin – both mean an Airman's drinking mug.

R/T. Radio telephony.

Rock-Ape. Member of RAF Regiment. Believed to have all been recruited from the colonies of their kind found on Gibraltar.

Ring, Losing your. Air-sick.

Round the bend. Noticeably pottier than ones contemporaries.

S.P. Service Police. And they say Hitler had no illegitimate children.

Stap Me! Expression of exasperation, from Captain Foulenough of *The Daily Mirror*.

Stuff it! No thanks!

Square-bashing. Foot Drill, Rifle Drill and "Alright Lads, fall out behind the Hanger for a smoke!"

Skive. Work-Dodging. Every erk was always looking out for a good one!

Short-arm Inspection. See FFI.

Squaddie. Shorthand for Squadron Leader.

Sprog. A sub-species of Erk. Recognizable by its green colour and lack of "savvy".

Sparks. Radio/wireless and Radar technicians. Considered themselves close to the ultimate in human evolution.

Shirley Temple. Vulgar enquiries as to whether you were suffering from the delusion that you were this child actress meant that you were making a chump of yourself!

Sally-Ann. Salvation Army, a voluntary organization that reached the spots the NAAFI couldn't reach!

Sky Pilot. Padre, irrespective of denomination they were A1 suppliers of fags and tea.

Stoned. (also 'screechers'). Incapable of coherent speech due to intake of too much alcohol. Most examples were seen on the evening of Golden Eagle Day.

Second Dicky. Possibly anatomical description of a second pilots redundancy. After all the First Pilot had got George.

Signing-on. Airmen having completed an engagement contracting for a further period were considered by their peers to be more pitied than blamed!

Shufti! Look! (Arabic)

Stores. There were Main Stores, Equipment Stores, etc, also run by power-mad maniacs they never had anything you wanted!

Trolley-Ack. Aircraft starter.

Trick-Cyclist. Psychiatrist. The person you had to persuade that you were further round the bend than he/she was (after all THEY didn't want to fly!).

Up the creek. This was a mythical location where it was possible to paddle so far as to be beyond help – worse still if you were without a paddle!

U/S. Unserviceable. Presently unfit for its purpose

Victory Vs. Cigarettes, allegedly made from Camel-dung. They were very common in the Mid-East. A major cause of homesickness.

Wingco. Wing Commander.

Win. To find something before it was lost!

Wizard. Super, spiffing and jolly good show!

Woods. Woodbines. Airman's preferred smoke. Type of dung used, a mystery!

"Where are you from?" asked the well-shrunk beret as we moved towards the tailgate.

"Padgate!" replied a raw (in more ways than one) recruit.

"Padgate, what?" demanded the beret.

"Er, er, Padgate Lancs," offered our man.

"What do you think these are?" roared our holiday guide, pointing to two stripes on his sleeve.

"Oh! Padgate, CORPORAL!"

"Yes, and don't you EVER forget it!"

The "beret" made our lives hell for the first few weeks, but we gradually found his bark was much worse than his bite, and he earned our respect and our affection. We could drill for him far better than for any other instructor for some unaccountable reason.

Alan Turner

OLD CUTFINGER

There were five huts in our Flight. We were told that the best hut on the Friday inspection would win the Flight radio for the week. Since there was only one radio per Flight, competition would be fierce.

It was our first week on "The Flights" and a council of war amongst our thirty hut members split the 'Bull-Night' communal tasks into teams. One group would do the ablutions, another the brown lino floor (rather than each man doing his own bedspace). Another team to blacken the stoves, another lampshades and windows, whilst yet another team was despatched to beg, borrow or steal sufficient cardboard to "square-up" big packs, small packs etc. (The consumption of Duraglit sky-rocketed!)

No team wanted either "Spike" Jones or "Old Cut-finger". Spike was good-hearted and would try anything he was asked to do, but could be guaranteed to make a cock of it, whatever it was! Cutfinger had pricked his finger on his bayonet, and had it bandaged in the Sick-Bay. His stock phrase was, "Because I've cut my finger, I can't bull my boots/do my brasses/clean my rifle/do up my webbing/polish my cap-badge/etc, etc."

So "Nottingham" did his brasses, "Kidder" scrubbed and blancoed his webbing, I bulled his boots, and the communal teams bulled his bedspace, polished his window brasses and cleaned his window. Our Senior man told Cutfinger and Spike just to do their personal kit, as their "helpers" would be busy. We were so keen to produce the best bulled hut that nobody went to the NAAFI on Thursday Nights except (as we later discovered) Cutfinger!

The first Friday parade arrived. The hut orderlies did a splendid final job – and we won the radio! The other huts reacted strongly, and after having enjoyed AFN's broadcasts for a week we were determined to keep it. So our hut went bull-mad! Even Spike gradually got the message and became a modest bull-expert, but after two weeks in which we managed to hold onto the radio – much to the other huts' chagrin – we were still responding to Cutfinger's pleas for help. Because he wouldn't pull his weight, the rest of us had to take responsibility for him and we were reluctant to say "Blow you Jack!" because if he let us down we would lose the radio.

One Friday morning we were all rushing round for the morning parade, checking each other's boots, greatcoats, webbing, rifles, rifle slings and bayonet frogs. When we were all dressed, Cutfinger was still standing by his bed with his greatcoat and webbing on, but none of it fastened.

"You haven't buttoned up!" exclaimed the Senior Man.

"I can't!" said Cutfinger, "because of my poorly finger!"

Two of us impatiently buttoned up his greatcoat, fastened his webbing, and with the ubiquitous yellow duster, wiped off any fingerprints on his brass and made certain he would pass muster.

On the way out to "Fall in on the road, come on move!" Cutfinger's bandage fell off! Those nearest to him saw that if there had ever been a wound on his finger it had long since healed!

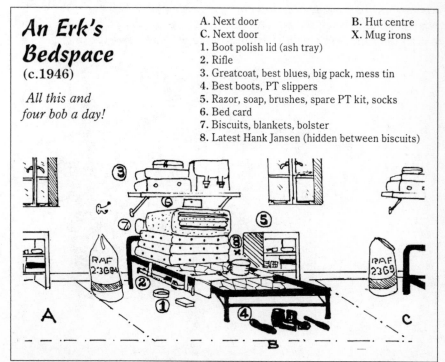

An Erk's Bedspace
(c.1946)

All this and four bob a day!

A. Next door   B. Hut centre
C. Next door   X. Mug irons
1. Boot polish lid (ash tray)
2. Rifle
3. Greatcoat, best blues, big pack, mess tin
4. Best boots, PT slippers
5. Razor, soap, brushes, spare PT kit, socks
6. Bed card
7. Biscuits, blankets, bolster
8. Latest Hank Jansen (hidden between biscuits)

For the rest of our stay at Padgate there were 29 friends in the hut... and Cutfinger. We felt that he'd used the rest of us, and that was hard to forgive.

Some 18 months later I was walking up towards the "Stonebow" in Lincoln and saw two RAFP's in full fig standing there. As I crossed the road to avoid them, I saw that one of them was old Cutfinger!

"Well," I thought, "as it says in the advert, there's a trade for everybody in the RAF!

R. Suppards

GOODBYE TO SQUARE-BASHING

After 16 weeks we could fire a rifle (Lee-Enfield Mk. III), stick a bayonet in a sack, fire a Sten (without shooting anyone we knew), and strip a Bren. We could carry out reasonably complicated Foot and Rifle drill, march in step and Bull up anything in sight.

We'd seen so many lurid American films about Social Diseases that many of us couldn't look a female in the face, and at least in theory we knew how to kill with our eating irons!

The next step was to be given our trades (except volunteers, who already knew what their next move was). Everyone had heard the story of the plumber who had been "trade-tested": the Examiner had reported 'Joint well done', but all the same the plumber was posted to St. Athan as a u/t Cook!

'AIRMAN! AM I 'URTIN' YOU?'
'NO, CORPORAL.'
'WELL, I SHOULD BE, I'M TREADIN' ON YER BACK 'AIR. GET IT CUT YOU 'AIRY LITTLE 'ORROR!'

WAS IT LIKE THIS FOR YOU?

Not at home on the range...

"COME ON SHIRLEY TEMPLE!" . . . . . "I 'OPE WE NEVER 'AVE TO GO TO WAR AGAINST SACKLAND!"

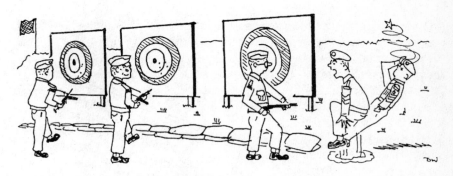

"CORPORAL, I ONLY GOT OFF THREE ROUNDS AND MY STEN HAS JAMMED!"

"I DIDN'T MISS, CORPORAL! I THINK THEY ALL WENT THROUGH THE SAME HOLE!"

WAS IT LIKE THIS FOR YOU?

Some of the Flight were to be Equippers, others were bound for trade training in Radar, Radio, Engines, Airframes, Accounts, or as Cooks or Medics. More than a few were keen to become PTIs, SPs or DIs. The unkind said that it was the Tapes they wanted! But most seemed reasonably content with the trade they'd been given.

The final Pass-Out Parade was carried out to a band which played "The Standard of St. George, The Royal Air Force March-past, and The General Salute.

Did anybody ever go on a Parade where the General Salute was given without singing under his breath as he held his gun at the Present:

> "Stand by your beds,
> Here comes the Air Vice Marshal,
> He's got rings upon his arm,
> But he's only got one ********"

An AVM taking the salute *must* be able to hear a 1000 Erks singing this less-than-complimentary version in unison! Most disconcerting!

The first posting was always the worst! The first snag was **Clearing**: Armoury, Laundry, Library, Stores, SWO's Office, PSI, Accounts and a hundred other places you'd never even heard of. But **Arriving** was even worse! You could normally reckon on a week either coming or going before you'd got all the signatures required!

And of course Movements would give you a list of changes which could leave you on Crewe station for the whole of Sunday... as well as sending you to the wrong unit!

"NAH MATE, NUMBER 3 RS IS AT _UPPER_ MUDDLECOMBE... 4 MILES DOWN THE ROAD....
NO TRANSPORT I'M AFRAID.... GOODNIGHT!"

WAS IT LIKE THIS FOR YOU?

CHAPTER II

Learning a Trade

Those who'd got a trade in Radar went to Yatesbury in bleakest Wiltshire. It was known as the Station with the biggest Parade Ground in the RAF. Rumour had it that there were squads out there still missing from the FIRST war.

It was also where a Flight Sergeant existed who was renowned for confusing anybody he ever gave an order to. For example, detailing fatigues to five U/t Radar Mechs.

"I want 'alf of yew to report to the Orficers' Mess, and 'alf of yew to report to 8 Wing NAAFI".

Now Radar Mechs can count, so the one in the middle said,

"Where shall I go, Flight Sergeant?"

To which our hero replied,

"Yew will keep your mouth SHUT, when addressing a Senior NCO!"

For those who worried about grasping the technology of what was then the infant science of Electronics their fears were allayed by the first lecture, known ever after as "Booing and Harking."

"If you are in a valley where there is an echo, you shout, 'Boo!' then hark for the echo. If you measure the time between booing and harking to the echo, and divide by two you have the time the sound took to travel to the reflecting surface. You know the speed of sound so you can calculate how far away the reflecting surface is.

So that's what Radar is, Booing and Harking!"

Months later, "Sparks" were awarded, and there was another Pass-out parade, another Clearance, and another posting. This time to an operational station. But now as a tradesman earning 5/6d per day, and with a new vocabulary.

'Browned off', 'Chokker' and 'fed up' all disappeared, with such expressions as 'Flippin' stroll on'. We were Radar Men now with our own words! There was...

Flippin' ro-tate. An expression of extreme disgust. This was derived from the Mobile Radar Units. If the Diesel that rotated the aerial broke down, an off-watch bod had to rotate the aerial by using a device like a push-bike and pedalling like mad. Radar men are not generally physical types – hence the disgust!

Around the Camp

"IT'S WHAT ME MUM USED TO LIFT ME OUT OF THE BATH WITH!"

"YOU HAVE NOT GOT A PAIN IN YOUR _ABDOMEN_, AIRMEN HAVE _STOMACHS!_"

"I WANT TWO VOLUNTEERS INTERESTED IN MUSIC."

SWO: "WOULD YOU LIKE A CUSHION?"

"IS THAT AN 'R' OR A 'P'?"

Cheesed to cut-off. Thermionic valves controlled throughput from anode to cathode by varying voltage applied to the grid. Too much "choke" and the valve 'cut-off' or became inert.

Scope Dope. Radar Operator.

Happidromes. A group of three radar equipments, Types 10, 11 & 12, which combined to give Height, Bearing, Range etc. Named for three comedians, Ramsbottom, Enoch and Lovejoy who were in a radio show called *Happidrome*.

...as well as all the Technical stuff that had passed through our ears into our notebooks without stopping on the way!

LANGUAGE PROBLEMS

YATESBURY 1947 AND THEREAFTER

On the first leg of Radar training at Nº 8 AGRS, our Theory course was given by a red-haired Corporal who hailed from Belfast with an Ulster accent that you could cut with a knife.

The first part of the course consisted of the explanation of pulse transmission and the advice that the symbol for Transmitter was TX. He gave notes very quickly, and it was necessary to take down his lectures in a Rough Book and copy out in "Fair-Hand", into the Note-Book in the evenings with properly drawn diagrams illustrated with coloured pencils. So effectively we were taking down straight dictation.

When he came to discuss the Receiver he called it something that sounded like *aurex* (well, it seemed reasonable – something to do with speech and hearing!). Imagine my surprise when I received my Best-Book (which I was quite proud of, because I thought it was immaculate) after marking to find a note in red ink – *9/10. Twit! See me!*

At the first opportunity I went up to his desk and said,

"You wanted to see me Corporal."

"Dats roight," he said, "You write Oar-ex as Oar-ex and not as Aurex!" I looked at him blankly.

"Look laddie!" and he wrote on a corner of my notebook... RX

"*Dats* Oar-ex!"

Well, I philosophised – you live and learn – but I didn't! Sometime later at 2 ANS as a student Navigator, we were being trained on the elements of airborne anti-submarine warfare. The Flying Officer Instructor had lost his two front teeth. I was alright taking notes on MAD Gear (Magnetic Detection) but when he got onto "Thonar Buoyth" (Sonar Buoys) I only just stopped myself getting *9/10 Twit! See me* in my notes again!

These days students are given typed notes... I wish they'd done it in my time! **R. Suppards**

WAS IT LIKE THIS FOR YOU?

During the War, many young Polish children found their way to what was then Persia to be brought up by the Free Poles. As they reached military age they were given the option amongst others of joining the Royal Air Force which Zygmund decided to accept. Part of their signals training was carried out at North Camp.

Zygmund spoke English with panache and flair but with little regard for grammar, so when a group of officers all of Air Rank came to inspect the camp, Zygmund's Flight Sergeant felt that it would be a kindness to all if he did not appear on the Parade because he ran the risk of confusing everybody. The Chiefy even suggested that Zygmund hid in a pile of old wooden Engine cases that had been dumped on the far side of the airfield.

The day of the inspection came. From his hideout, Zygmund could hear the band playing the Polish National Anthem, then the RAF March-past. The sun came out and Zygmund lay back in the sunshine relaxed and at peace with the world.

Around 15.00 hrs, he found he'd smoked all his cigarettes and was beginning to feel hungry. He decided to see what was going on across the airfield. On all fours he carefully crept around the side of the crate he'd been hiding in. He put his hand on an immaculately polished shoe, then saw that there was an officer's blue trouser leg above it, then he saw that he was on all fours in front of an Air Commodore, with a number of officers behind, followed by his own Flight Sergeant.

The Air Commodore looked down at Zygmund, still on all fours

"What the blazes do you think you're doing man?" he roared.

Most of Zygmund's English had deserted him in his hour of need, but one phrase came bubbling to the top.

"I'm looking for zings, Sir".

"What sort of things?" asked the Air Commodore.

"I don't know, Sir" admitted our hero.

The Air Commodore with something of a twinkle in his eye said,

"Flight Sergeant, this airman seems to be in some difficulty – take his name and then find out what his problem is, will you?"

The entourage moved on. "I'll tell you what the trouble is," hissed the F/ Sgt. "you won't bloody learn English!"

"But," said Zygmund, "vot else could I have zed?"

"You wouldn't have had to say a word if your English had been good enough to go on the parade!"

Two years later I met Zygmund at Waddington where he told me this story – by then he spoke excellent English!   *R. Suppards*

ESCAPE FROM JUSTICE

It was amazing how in the RAF there were times when out of a clear blue sky you were suddenly and unexpectedly treated to a shower of (you know what!) and other times when you knew a whole barrow-load should fall on your richly deserving head nothing happened. It was almost as though Newton's Law (what goes up must come down) was suspended at random by some Superior Being's whim.

An early personal observation was whilst I was on the Fitter IIa course at Cosford. Suddenly there was a blitz on Bull-Nights where the powers that be seemed to be demanding a return to the Bull standards of square-bashing days. The difference to us erks was that at square-bashing there was nothing much else to do but bull, but at Cosford our prime objective was to learn about airframes, and there was considerably less interest and less time available for needless bull.

But you had to do sufficient to keep out of trouble. Tuesday night was bull night, and CO's Parade followed on Wednesday mornings.

I was the Senior Man in our hut, and I and another bod stayed behind for a few minutes to put the last touches to the hut.

"OK," we agreed, "its as good as its going to be, lets go!"

We put on our greatcoats and I slung my gas-mask over my shoulder ... PLUNK! I'd hit the Fire Extinguisher dead on the nose!

Panic stations! The two of us got the Fire Extinguisher outside and went to work with mop and bucket. But two erks in five minutes can nowhere nearly undo the ravages made by a determined attack from a provoked Fire Extinguisher.

ERK'S NIGHTMARE: *"COME ON! WE'RE ON PARADE IN FIVE MINUTES AND YOU'RE BILLET ORDERLY!"*

WAS IT LIKE THIS FOR YOU?

My problem was that if the CO found the hut below standard it meant loss of privileges for everyone in the hut. So that I, as Senior Man with the added responsibility of keeping the other hut members out of the stuff I mentioned earlier, had in fact succeeded in dropping them all in it!

The day in classes dragged interminably, and I couldn't concentrate on the lectures, dreading to find a note from the SWO when we got back to the hut from classes. But there was nothing!

Some of the blokes, as they came into the hut made rude comments about the perils of having as a Senior Man someone who could be left in charge of a moderately well-bulled hut and in five minutes completely foul it up – but that was all!

Did the CO fail to see the mess we'd left behind? Impossible! Did he see the mess, guess what had happened, and charitably overlook it? Even more impossible! So as Sherlock Holmes said, "If you dismiss everything else, what remains – no matter how incredible must be the truth."

All that was left was the certainty that the CO had not set foot in our hut. Newton's Law had been suspended once again. So one could surmise that even the CO was not above the odd bit of skiving.

We decided not to delude ourselves into believing that we had discovered a new Natural Law – that "the CO *never* inspects our hut" so we decided to bull-up on Bull Nights. But I created Dee's Law, "From now on I will be very careful around fire extinguishers".

Bernard Dee

SWO'S WORKING PARADE

'I WANT ALL THE BEDS IN THESE 'UTS DISMANTLED, TAKEN OUTSIDE AND MANTLED UP AGAIN!'

WAS IT LIKE THIS FOR YOU?

An Airman's Lot

23.59 DECEMBER 31ST .... WELL, SOMEBODY HAD TO DO IT!

ERK'S DILEMMA: "IF I SALUTE HIM AND HE TRIES TO ACKNOWLEDGE HE FALLS OFF HIS BIKE... BUT IF I DON'T...."

"WHO SPREAD THE BUTTER ON THIS BREAD?"

"I DID! ... ANY COMPLAINTS?"

"YES FLIGHT SERGEANT... SOMEBODY'S SCRAPED IT OFF AGAIN!"

WAS IT LIKE THIS FOR YOU?

CHAPTER III

Operational on a Bomber Station

The secret of success in the RAF was to do your job well, and provided you kept your bedspace tidy, didn't upset the NCOs or get across the SWO, life could be quite pleasant.

The great thing was to try to remain anonymous. Some people spent their time trying this by most extraordinary means (see cartoon right), but others sought rank by any or all means at their disposal (see below)!

OVERHEARD IN THE HANGER:

"THE NEXT MAN WHO CALLS ME CHIEFY, I SHALL DO SOMETHING UNSPEAKABLE TO!"

(FALSETTO VOICES FROM ABOVE.)
"CHIEFY, CHIEFY, CHIEFY!"

"GOOD MORNING FLIGHT SERGEANT, I'VE GOT A LITTLE SPARROW FOR YOUR CAT!"

WAS IT LIKE THIS FOR YOU?

FRIENDSHIP, AIR-FORCE STYLE

I passed out from 2 RS Yatesbury as a Radar Mech and was posted the next day to Waddington. It was my 19th birthday, and the day before Pay Parade at Yatesbury. I arrived at Waddington too late for supper in the Mess, and I was flat broke. I was given a bed in the Signals billet, drew blankets, wearily made my pit down, and threw myself on to it. Talk about brassed off! I hadn't eaten since breakfast, and tomorrow I would have to "Arrive", try to arrange a supplementary Pay Parade, report to my new Section on a new Station where it had been snowing all day! Flippin' Roll On!

The bed on one side was empty, and on the other side sat a bloke bulling his boots. He gave them a last loving polish with a yellow duster and then looked across at me.

"I'm just going over to the NAAFI for supper. If you'd like to come with me I can show you where it is."

"Thanks," I said, "but I'm skint!"

"That's alright," he smiled, "I've got five bob, I'll lend you a couple of bob for your supper."

I paid him back as soon as I was paid, and a couple of weeks later he was posted. That's all I remember about him, except that he was nicknamed "Banjo" and that he was a Ground Wireless Mech.

But that was the Air Force. Unlike the Navy, where they served in the same ship for ages, and the Army where they stayed together in the same Battalion, we were posted as individuals. You made friends at Square-bashing, but the Flight was dispersed to the four winds as we went to Trade training, then after Pass-Out dispersed again to new Stations – almost always alone.

It was no different with Aircrew training. Pilots and Navigators started off together at ITS then they split to their different schools, then soon after 'Wings' they were split again to Command training and dispersed to the Squadrons. So it was unusual to stay for any length of time with the same bunch of bods. You learned how to make friends very quickly, share your last five bob with someone, like Banjo did with me, and then say goodbye and forget the old friends as soon as they passed cut of your life. It made little difference if they just got posted or the chop.

At the time you could not keep all their memories warm, and only the closest people remained clear in your memory. How often did you find yourself saying to someone you felt was, like you, 'an old hand', "What was the name of that bloke who accidentally spilt whitewash all over the SWO?" – only to discover that the other 'old hand' had only arrived *after* the event – and to discover you were the only one who remembered it?

Was this, I wonder, one reason why RAF wit was quicker and our sense of humour different to that of the Army and Navy?   *R. Suppards*

AN EARLY NATIONAL SERVICE EXPERIENCE (c. Feb '49.)

Some weeks after completing square bashing on N⁰ 2 Wing, Padgate, I was given my first posting to St. Athan. A temporary bed was found for me on that first night. During the night I was awakened by a gentle tap on the shoulder. On coming-to I found myself staring into a face thrust close to mine, and what a face! It was a real pugilist's mug, with a broken nose, cauliflower ear, a black eye, and plaster on one cheekbone. In a surprisingly gentle tone, the face informed me that I was sleeping in his bed, but that it was OK for me to stay there for the rest of the night!

In the morning I learned that the bed I'd been given belonged to the heavyweight boxing champion of the RAF who had returned unexpectedly early from a bout in Germany!   *John H. Drew*

WHAT GOES AROUND, COMES AROUND

I was a Sergeant Fitter IIE stationed at East Kirby which was shared by 57 and 630 Squadrons in 1944. On the night of 7/8th May both squadrons attacked Tours. One of 'my' Lancasters was DXL, No. JB723 of 57 Squadron.

On its bombing run it was intercepted by a night-fighter and badly shot-up. It struggled back to the UK with a wounded rear gunner aboard. Unable to make East Kirby, it made an Emergency Landing at Tarrant Rushden in deepest Dorset.

With the exception of the rear gunner, Sgt W.W.J. Carver, who was rushed off to hospital, the rest of the crew, F/O R.F. Walker (Pilot), F/o H.B. MacKinnon (Navigator), F/o K E. Bay (Air Bomber) P/o T. Quale (M/U), Sgt E. Chung (Flt Eng), Flt Sgt R.A. Hammersley (WOP/AG) returned to East Kirby the following day.

Some days elapsed whilst we waited for a damage report and to find a lull in the workload, before a party of fitters and allied trades, with myself as NCO i/c were ordered to Tarrant Rushden to repair DXL.

We were driving a Bedford 30 cwt, with a Port-Outer engine chained down on the back. The further South we drove the more congested the roads became, with Army convoy after convoy all heading in the same direction!

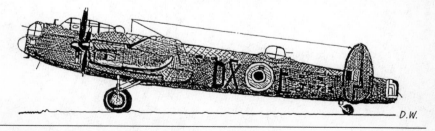

On a clear stretch of road near Salisbury, an American tank transporter, complete with a 40-ton Sherman tank aboard shot past us going at a ferocious rate of knots, driven by two very cool and relaxed looking black US soldiers. They were travelling so fast I thought for a second we'd *stopped!*

My driver looked at me and raised an eyebrow. Answering the unspoken question, I said, "Not to worry, with these winding roads, we'll pass *them* in another few miles!" I was more right than I knew. Some four miles further on we did pass them! They'd gone through a hedge and turned over, and were surrounded by a group of very cross looking US Army police (the Americans never did really master driving on our roads!).

It was pitch dark when we arrived at Tarrant Rushden, and we were closely questioned by the SPs who showed the greatest reluctance to let us in. They just could not seem to believe that we had turned up to repair DXL on this night of all nights, in fact they seemed to prefer to think that we were a bunch of German saboteurs!

We were still waiting to go to find DXL when the Tannoy bawled out, *"The Initial Landings have been successful!"* We had been carrying out our duty completely oblivious to the fact that we were at the heart of the final preparations for D-Day! (Nobody had told us what was going on.) In fact during that night a large part of the Glider force had been launched from Tarrant Rushden, and during the day we saw further waves of Horsa gliders being towed out to Normandy.

Forty-three years had passed since that incident when in July 1987 my wife and I went to 57 and 630's Squadron Reunion. We were chatting to another couple in the hotel where we staying, talking about where we were on D-Day. Nearby was another couple apparently deep in a conversation of their own until the man must have overheard me mention DXL, because he

SPRING IN LINCOLNSHIRE...

"....I'D RATHER 'ANG AROUND THE 'DILLY UNDERGROUND AND LIVE OFF THE EARNINGS OF A HIGH BORN LADY...."

leaned over to me and said, "Thanks for changing the engine on our Lanc!" It turned out that he'd been the Navigator on DXL, and later that day he introduced us to his WOP/AG.

I was glad I hadn't held my breath waiting all those years for those words of thanks – but I was delighted to find that they, like me, were still going strong.

Frank Beasley

NOTHING LIKE BEING ON THE WRONG END!

On the 18th of July 1944, 57 and 630 Squadrons based at East Kirby laid on a Maximum Effort for a Mass Daylight raid on Caen, in support of "Operation Goodwood," which was the code-name for a major British and Canadian attack to take Caen. Both squadrons put up 17 aircraft, and they all returned safely.

Nearly a 1,000 bombers took part in this attack. At the end of July leave for ground staff was recommenced, and I was one of the lucky ones granted leave first!

To start my journey home from East Kirby I had first to get to Lincoln, and I'd hardly stepped outside the Camp Gates when a Captain in the Para's pulled up and asked, "Where are you bound for, Sergeant?"

I gave him one of my best salutes and replied, "Lincoln, Sir!"

"Hop in," he replied, "I'm going all the way."

As we chatted he asked me if I'd been on the Caen raid. It was a fair enough question as you couldn't hide forty-odd Lancasters on an airfield. So I told him, no, I was a Sgt Fitter i/c Maintenance, but "my" two Squadrons had put 34 Lancs over the target.

He then told me that on the morning of the 18th he'd been doing a "recce" on the German side of the bomb line when he'd looked up to see the best

THE JANKER WALLAH'S TALE

...SO CHURCHILL SAID TO THE KING, "I FINK THAT BUGGER MONTY IS ARTER MY JOB!" "FANK GAWD FOR THAT!" SAYS THE KING " I FORT 'E WAS ARTER MINE!"....

part of a thousand bombers coming his way, in wave after wave – all with their bomb doors open!

When the bombs started to fall he described the absolute hell of noise and flying debris which engulfed him, and then he observed, "I don't know how Jerry felt, but only myself and my laundry know how terrified I was!"

It was very gratifying to receive such a fulsome and unsolicited testimonial as to the effectiveness of 'my' two squadrons – amongst others of course – but the Para Captain was a jolly good type and I was glad they'd all missed him!

Frank Beasley

A GRISLY TALE

We have all heard the horror stories of the National Servicemen, who, coming from a sheltered upbringing at home, could not "hack it" and committed suicide, usually by hanging. I was a witness to one such case and will relate the tale to you.

My bedspace was one of thirty in a room on the upper floor of a four-roomed, two-storey barrack block, which was situated by the side of the road that surrounded the Parade Square of RAF Upwood, Huntingdonshire.

At the time, Upwood was a fully operational bomber command station of 3 Group, and hosted three squadrons of Avro Lincolns (the uprated version of the faithful Lancaster). These 'Lincs' were involved in the anti Mau-Mau campaign in Kenya and each squadron was rotated in turn on a six-weekly basis.

POWER CORRUPTS – 1

'THAT WING COMMANDER ONLY ADDRESSED ME AS SERGEANT FOUR TIMES!. ROUTE HIS TRAVEL WARRANT LINCOLN–PORTSMOUTH VIA GLASGOW, EDINBURGH AND CARDIFF!'

WAS IT LIKE THIS FOR YOU?

Life at Upwood was fairly gentle, peaceful and above all calm. The discipline was not extreme and as long as you performed your duties adequately, you were left well alone.

Upon the cessation of the anti Mau-Mau hostilities the Lincs were returned to base and subsequently grounded. They were replaced by the twin jet engined English Electric Canberra bomber.

With the advent of these high speed aircraft, life became rather fraught and the speed of life increased threefold. Trying to keep up with them proved to be rather nerve-wracking. Many problems arose due to the fact that much of the ground equipment was only uprated to match the aircraft in dribs and drabs.

Night flying training became the norm with, as a consequence, disturbed sleep patterns. It was around 7am one morning, when the washrooms in the barrack block were in full spate, beds being hastily made up and nobody could find a broom (memories are made of this), when one of the hardier characters in the room flung open the window at the head of his bed to clear the "fug".

"Bloody Hell!" he exclaimed, "Quick! Look out there!"

Those of us still in the room dashed to our own windows and quickly opened them. The sight that met our eyes was of a body, wearing complete battle dress, beret and, ludicrously, a pair of issue Wellington boots with the tops turned down.

The body was suspended by the neck from a low branch of one of the trees situated on the edge of the 'square'. It was spinning very slowly in a gentle breeze, its head slumped over to one side because of the rope around the neck

POWER CORRUPTS – 2

"SORRY MATE, WE HAVEN'T GOT ANY SIZE 12S...
WOULD THREE PAIRS OF SIZE FOURS DO?"

WAS IT LIKE THIS FOR YOU?

"Quick!" someone shouted, "We've got to cut him down!"

We all thundered down the stone staircase, drawing those in the washrooms with us. As we rushed across the grass at the edge of the square, the first arrivals, on approaching close to the body, pulled up short and – very callously – burst out laughing! What was hanging from the branch was a very well made dummy with a "bolster" for a head .A notice pinned to the front of the battle-dress said: *This is a leaving present from one national serviceman who has finished his time. Good luck, suckers!*   **Mike Harrison**

SURPRISE! SURPRISE!   FELTWELL 1941

For some reason or other, the MO didn't want on this particular occasion to trail all around the barrack blocks carrying out routine FFIs. The letters stood for 'free from infection' and required a more or less routine inspection of an airman's intimate parts to ensure that the subject was free from 'social diseases'. I suppose he got as bored with it as we did! Presumably to save time one day, Squadron Orders stated:

All Squadron Ground Staff personnel will parade in N⁰· 1 Hanger at 09.30 for an FFI.

A Flight, B Flight and Maintenance duly fell in and were marched to the NAAFI, where the inspections were due to take place. We recognised this as a bit of luck, because it meant that, after the inspection was over, we would be first in the NAAFI, as it opened at 10 o'clock and it was a case of "first come, first served."

We entered, marching in a column of threes halted and right-turned facing the six shuttered hatches of the servery. One sold tobacco and sweets, another writing materials, Duraglit and dusters, the others served tea and wads.

At 09.45 the Squadron Warrant Officer gave the order, "Drop your slacks and pants and raise your shirts and vests!"

We stood there, exposed to the fresh air. Outside there were a queue of erks already beginning to form in anticipation of the NAAFI opening, being kept out by SPs.

The MO walked into the NAAFI to carry out the inspection, but at the same time the six shutters were raised, and behind them stood six NAAFI girls ready to start selling. The girls eyes bulged in disbelief as they beheld the sight before them, and then the shutters slammed down again to the accompaniment of their cries of shock and embarrassment. One can only guess at what may have been their thoughts and feelings on witnessing such a spectacle! I know one thing though, some of the chaps in the front row were very reluctant to go to the NAAFI afterwards and look those girls in the eye!   **Frank Beasley**

It was a Saturday afternoon, and Waddington had been made a Master Diversion Unit, which meant that Flying Control Staff always manned the Tower. I was on the afternoon watch. There wasn't an aircraft in the sky. Through the open windows I could smell the grass on the airfield and hear larks singing. I could see the F/Lt Flying Controller sitting behind his glass window gently dozing in the warm sun. The sky was clear apart from odd patches of fair-weather cumulus. Suddenly our peace was disturbed by an aircraft calling up Waddington:

"Waddington Tower from Grouser Two-Six. How do you read please?"

The Flying Control Officer jumped to wakefulness and looked back at me. He had no need to worry, I knew what the Grouser call-sign meant. It would be an Anson crewed by very experienced, high-ranking aircrew who, on duty with an Air Ministry Unit, prowled around the country carrying out landings or overshoots to test the efficiency of reaction, and the speed of the Emergency Services. They liked to report unfavourably if they could.

Quick as a flash I replied, "Grouser Two-Six from Waddington Tower. Receiving you strength five. Pass your Message. Over."

They replied by requesting landing instructions, which I gave them. The gist of it was they were required to enter the airfield circuit at a 1000 feet, and when they turned to line up with the threshold of the runway-in-use, they were to tell us they were on Finals.

The Flying Controller moved the Ambulance and Fire truck onto the Apron and we waited for the Grouser to appear in circuit. There was not a

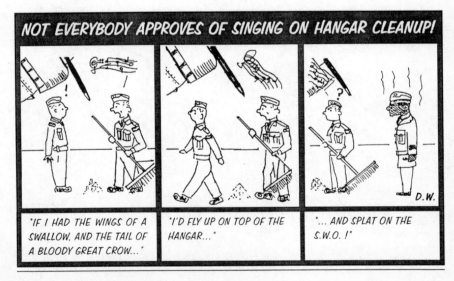

NOT EVERYBODY APPROVES OF SINGING ON HANGAR CLEANUP!

"IF I HAD THE WINGS OF A SWALLOW, AND THE TAIL OF A BLOODY GREAT CROW..."

"I'D FLY UP ON TOP OF THE HANGAR..."

"... AND SPLAT ON THE S.W.O.!"

sign! Then he called "On Finals". Unless the aircraft was invisible, it wasn't on *our* field!

Next the Grouser Pilot called up, "I am in front of your Tower where are the Emergency Services?" The snottiness of his criticism stung even over the R/T.

I replied, "Grouser, our Emergency Equipment *is* in front of the Tower on the Apron!"

The Flying Control Officer was beside himself with glee.

"They must have landed on our disused Satellite!" he chortled.

We didn't hear from them again for a while and I assumed they must have discovered their mistake.

Some half hour later I heard, "Cranwell Tower from Grouser Two-Six, how do you read please?"

They were still transmitting on our Local Frequency which meant that only we could hear them, Cranwell couldn't.

"Sir, I said to the Flying Control Officer, "Should I tell Grouser they've got to change frequency to call up Cranwell?"

"No, better not," he said, "they'll know that they landed at the satellite thinking they were at Waddington. If we told them they'd just made another Air Discipline blunder they might think we were taking the mickey! Just log them calling up Cranwell and leave it at that."

We went back to contemplating the lovely Spring afternoon.

R. Suppards

AN AIRMAN'S LOT — 1

"SORRY LADS, SOLD OUT!. BYE!"

A NASTY TURN

(National Service 1948–50)

A party of very green erks, myself included, were detailed to guard a bomb-dump which was on the runway at Rhoose. When not actually on guard we were allowed to rest in the guardroom. As "new boys" we were pretty much in awe of the "old hands".

It had always been drummed into us at square-bashing that playing cards for money was a serious offence, which could, if you were caught at it, lead to disciplinary action not excluding the "glass-house" – but a group of "old hands" were sitting around the table in the guardroom with money on the table, playing cards, fags in faces, gambling away like mad!

We watched fascinated. Then the "green" erks saw a ferocious-looking South Wales police-helmet (silver spike, chains and cap-badge) glide past the top of the frosted windows of the guardroom which faced onto the road.

"Cripes, now the card-players are for it!" we thought. Visions of being called as witnesses – or even being accused of playing ourselves and being hauled off to the "glasshouse" went through our minds.

We heard the sound of a bicycle being leaned against an outside wall. The door opened and in came this big, ruddy South Wales police constable. We froze! He looked round at the card-players.

"Everything alright lads?" he asked.

"All OK!" replied one of the players.

"Jolly good," said the constable, "I'll be off then. Cheerio!"

We heard his bike recede into the distance. The sun shone, the card players carried on, and we relaxed. Queer place, the Air Force! **John H. Drew**

(A.M.O.) – "AIR MECHANICS SHOULD FLY ON AIR TESTS"

D.W.

"REPORTING FOR AIR TEST, SIR".

"I BET 50% OF THE PEOPLE ON THE DECK THOUGHT WE WERE GOING TO CRASH!"

"50% OF THE PEOPLE UP HERE WERE BLOODY SURE OF IT!"

GET SOME TIME IN!

The Old Hands expected a measure of deference from that lowest of God's creations... The Sprog! Whilst often the sprog was in the same trade and quite possibly held the same rank, he just didn't have any time in. This attitude was encouraged by the Daily Rates of Pay. For example in 1941 a Parachute Packer was a Group V Trade, and pay was as follows:

Aircraftsman 2nd Class .... 2/- per day
Aircraftsman 2nd Class (over one year) ....2/9d per day
Aircraftsman 2nd Class (over two years) .... 3/- per day
Aircraftsman 1st Class .... 3/6d per day.
Leading Aircraftsman .... 4/- per day

Thus the Old Hands wanted to impress the Sprogs with their greater skills gained (and rewarded) for lengths of service.

So, an Old Hand might say to a Sprog who ventured an opinion: "Look Laddie, before you say things like that you ought to get your number dry!" or, "Get your knees Brown!"

Then there were the non-specific claims for Long Service such as...

1. When I joined the Air-Works, we didn't need numbers, we all knew each other!
2. Look mate, I was in the Air Force before the Dead Sea reported sick!
3. I was in the Air Force before Mortis became a Rigger!
4. I was in the mob before Pontius became a pilot!
5. There were only two ranks when I joined, AC2s and Group Captains!
6. We didn't have aeroplanes when I joined, only kites and balloons!
7. The navigation lights on the kites were lit by oil when I joined.

Then there were the put-downs...

"Call that a number? Its more like the population of China!"

And the cruelest one of all:

"Honestly! You're so effing useless you couldn't pour piss out of an old Wellington boot with a hole in the toe and the instructions written on the leg!"

The Old Hand would then demonstrate with great finesse exactly how it should be done.

The Adventures of A/c Plonk

"WELL SIR, I WAS CLEANING MY RIFLE..."

"HOW DO YOU KNOW WHEN IT'S FULL, SERGEANT?"

WAS IT LIKE THIS FOR YOU?

More Adventures of A/c Plonk

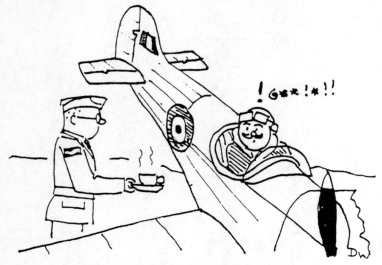

"I THOUGHT YOU MIGHT LIKE A CUP OF TEA, SIR!"

"OH FLIGHT SERGEANT, COME AND SEE WHT I'VE FOUND!"

CHAPTER IV

Other Commands – Same Cap Badge

The Navy used to have a saying, "Other ships, other cap-bands", which was their short-hand way of describing the differences between serving on a "Battle-waggon" as against a corvette.

Many of our members served in different Commands at different times: Fighter, Bomber, Coastal, Transport, Training etc., but the accounts in this section are from people who were not serving in Bomber Command at the time their accounts date from.

Most accounts in this section are from the unsung backwaters of Fighter Command, but there is one account where the writer had good cause to wonder:-

(A) Was he in the RAF at all?

(B) Perhaps the Air Force was trying to tell him something!

(C) Although he was (and still is) quite sure he originates from Somerset its quite possible that one of the Power Mad Maniacs (we have all suffered the vagaries of Records) had decided that Somerset was a suburb of Chicago, because no matter what Sid said or did, they insisted he was an American!

These accounts come in the main from the RAF's small ships – but we all wore the same cap-badge (whether or not you polished behind it was very much a matter of what "ship" you were serving on!).

"THAT'S A JU88, CORP!"   *"NAH... IT'S A BEAU."*   *"TOLD YER CORP!"*

WAS IT LIKE THIS FOR YOU?   **47**

LODGING AT THE PRIORY

The Central School of Aircraft Recognition, in which I was fortunate enough to serve for the major part of my National Service, was a small "lodger" unit, at this time located at Headquarters Fighter Command, Bentley Priory. All the instructors were NCOs, or were commissioned, and (with one notable exception) earned the respect due to their ranks, which contributed to a happy, but not sloppy unit.

On one occasion, two Corporals were visiting the Unit, and one of the instructors requested that I rustle up some coffee for the visitors. I duly took the coffee along to the Instructors' Room and went in, looking for the Corporals. The CO happened to be standing by the door, and as I entered he asked me what I wanted.

"I am looking for the two gentlemen who wanted the coffee, Sir."

"Turner, those are Corporals! They are *not* gentlemen. You must realise that in the Royal Air Force *nobody* below the rank of Sergeant is a gentleman! When you are demobbed next November, you can tell us all to go and get stuffed, but until then you must remember that!" There were roars of laughter around the room and a broad smile across the CO's face.

•

It was normal practice for us to wear civvies when working on a Saturday morning. One such morning, our Flight Sergeant Instructor was talking to a (uniformed) colleague when I hove into view on my way to the CSAR. I was wearing a navy blue blazer with RAF buttons on it. Result? – A snappy salute and a "Good Morning, Sah!" from the F/Sgt's companion.

Our Flight Sergeant did not enlighten his companion, but derived great amusement afterwards when telling his fellow instructors that the Orderly Room SAC had been saluted by, of all people, the *Station Warrant Officer!*

•

Nobody liked being on Fire Picquet. One night I was despatched to look for an officer who was required urgently. His exact whereabouts were unknown, but I was told that probably he had a room in the Officers' Quarters. This was unknown territory to me, and I was anxious not to 'drop a clanger'. I found my way into a corridor with names on the doors, whose exalted rank made me feel that I was on hallowed ground, but none of them bore the name of my quarry. What I needed was an erk who could give me a 'steer', but there was no sign of a duty orderly or a passing batman.

Then my eyes lighted on a door with a name-plate 'A/C Xxxx'. I reckoned this might be the orderly, Aircraftsman Xxxx.

I knocked. A voice bid me enter. It was a mature voice, and I *knew* I'd got it wrong. Wishing that I could turn and flee, I entered to find myself in a well

You Just Couldn't Win!

'I TOOK THE SERGEANT'S MESS TURKEY FOR A LARK SIR'

'CHARGE PUT BACK FOR AN OPTICIAN'S REPORT...'

'MORE SALT!'

'MORE SALT!'

'GREAT HEAVENS MAN! FAR TOO MUCH SALT!'

appointed room with a neatly folded uniform at the foot of a bed which contained a middle-aged gentleman sitting up and reading a book.

What on earth can you say, and retain your dignity, to the Senior Medical Officer of Fighter Command when you've just mistaken him for a batman, and an Air Commodore for an Aircraftsman?"

I was indeed, red-faced. Fortunately he was not the least worried by my intrusion upon his privacy. I gabbled something rapidly, bade him "Good night", saluted smartly and fled!

I never did locate the officer I'd been sent to find! **Alan Turner**

ROUGH JUSTICE!

Whilst stationed at Quedgely, Gloucester in the winter of 1943, I was sent as part of a guard detail to Moreton Vallence vehicle park. I drew the 10–12 duty, and was in the sentry box when I observed a westward-bound vehicle which stopped near the Gate. I took no action. Some 15 to 20 minutes later, the same vehicle, now going eastwards, pulled up outside the gate again. I immediately shouted,

"Halt! Who goes there!"

The reply? "The Orderly Officer!"

I replied with the time-honoured response,

"Advance and be recognised!"

However, he accused me of having been asleep when he passed me going Westwards, and asked what I would have done if he had fired a shot at me. Straight in with both feet I answered, "Do you think I'd have been fool enough to just stand here and let you do it?"

Result? Seven days 'CC' at Quedgley for insubordination to an officer!

Sid Arscott

FROM A GREAT HEIGHT

RAF Dimlington was a Type 54 Coastal Radar Station on the North-East coast of Yorkshire. It was November 1948, and the Airlift was in full swing. The station was working a three shift watch system, so it was on the air 24 hours a day. Demob had been stopped since August because of the National Emergency, and six of the total complement of thirty should have already departed. But that wasn't all. Orders had been given that off-watch personnel were to undergo a refresher course on Ground Combat training and to dig weapon pits and site machine guns. The reason was that the Coastal Radar was providing defensive support to the streams of aircraft flying to Berlin, and it was feared that Russian Commandos might try to take the Radar Stations out. They were to be defended. Since the total complement was thirty airmen, one officer, three NCOs and no other Air Force or Army support for some thirty miles, people felt a trifle lonely!

But feelings were heightened when a combined USAF/RAF exercise was announced. This was to take 48 hours and was to test the efficiency of the Northern Radar Chain.

As soon as it was dark, Bomber Command aircraft started showing up on our screens heading for Hull. The first night was ultra-hectic, with the screens flooded with Hostiles, Unidentifieds and Friendlies. Dawn came, and with it a lull. The screens were clear. It was a long established routine after a night underground in the Ops Block, drinking tea and sweating over the sets, to come up into the fresh sea air, walk to the cliff edge (the cliffs were 80ft high at this point) and "take a leak".

So Jock and Taff walked to the cliff edge to "ease springs". In no time at all they came racing back, saying, "Report a visual. Two Spitfires flying below the level of the cliffs, heading South!" The report was immediately passed to Filter Ops.

"Ah," said Chiefy, "they must be 'enemy' aircraft evading our radar."

"Well, they didna get away Scot free," said Jock. "I think I got one of 'em!"

R. Suppards

CHARGES OF DIFFERENT SORTS

At Church Lawford we were in Nissen Huts. There was a strip of lino down the centre of the hut, but the beds stood on concrete, and sweeping your bedspace raised enough dust off the concrete to make a fair representation of a Sahara sandstorm. The Discip Sergeant wanted to charge one of the hut-members with having a dirty bedspace because he'd found a piece of fluff under his bed. Nobody could figure out how he'd been able to distinguish the fluff from the dust!

Somebody in the Orderly Room had more sense than the Sergeant, because the charge was dropped. But a few days later the hut next door was on a different sort of charge. During the night some sort of electrical fault had developed, and we were aroused by shouts for help coming from our

OH YEAH?   NO SUCH LUCK!

"CPL JONES MISHEARD ME SIR...
I SAID BULLOCKS!"

"RATHER THAN 7 DAYS CC SIR,
COULDN'T I JUST BE SACKED?"

WAS IT LIKE THIS FOR YOU?

stricken neighbours. The steel walls of their hut had become electrified, and no-one in the hut could get out. They spent nearly all day huddled together in the middle of the hut, not daring to move until the electrical fault could be repaired.

We got yet a different charge when one of Billy Butlin's red monoplanes force-landed on our disused airfield, only to learn that nobody knew where the Station Fire Engine was!

The Friday CO's parade took place on the main runway. The Flights already on Parade could see snake-like columns marching around the peri-track from miles away! Giggles from the Flights already formed up rose to roars of laughter as the last Flight (running dangerously late) and marching at a very quick pace hove into view. The Flight Commander was REALLY corpulent, and his arms were swinging like windmills, but the supernumerary officer at the rear of the flight was diminutive! He was running at the double to keep up! It really lightened the burden of CO's Parade on that particular Friday Morning!   *John H. Drew*

NO TOAST, THANKS!   RAF RINGSTEAD, AUTUMN 1947

Ringstead was just like any other Radar Station – miles from anywhere! During the war, Radar stations were strictly "single sex units". The average complement was some 40 bods. As the RAF had to readjust to peacetime, many of the stations which formerly had been WAAF Stations reverted to RAF manning.

At Ringstead the WAAF moved out on a Wednesday and the RAF moved in the following day. A few days later there was an AOC's Inspection. Everybody not on duty stood by their beds for a hut inspection. In one hut, the occupants had beaten all the other huts to the punch by "winning" a small stove that they'd found in the Ablutions. It now held pride of place in the hut centre by the coke bunker, flanked by the two standard stoves.

As the AOC swept through the hut followed by his entourage, the Senior WAAF Officer stopped by one of the airmen and asked him what the little stove was doing there.

He replied, "We found it in the Ablutions Ma'am when we arrived and we use it for making toast." (On the radar stations there were no NAAFIs, and only one liberty a week, so supper was toast.)

The WAAF Officer stared at the airman for what seemed like a full minute, then she sniggered and went to speak to the Squadron Leader, who whispered to the Flight Lieutenant, who told the Flight Sergeant to get it returned to Stores immediately.

After the AOCs inspection was over, some of the hut members complained to the F/Sgt, who was a Scot, about the confiscation of their little stove and he said, "Do you innocent gommerils not know what the wimmin burned in yon little furnace?"

They shook their heads... so he told them.

All radar stations were connected indirectly by landline and in a week even the furthest units in the Northern Signals Area had heard about it... but it was only Ringstead where toast for supper was off the menu!

R. Suppards

OVERTIME PAY IN THE AIR FORCE?   RAF TANGMERE 1944

Tangmere was the Central Fighter Establishment in the Autumn of 1944 and I was working in the Carpenters Shop making templates when the Workshop Warrant Officer asked if there were any specialists in French Polishing. There was only one-me!

The airfield had been well bombed in 1940 and 1941 and there was a lot of rebuilding going on, including a new Officers Mess. Our carpenters had built

OBEY ORDERS WITH DISCRETION...

"YES SIR, I'M ON FIRE PIQUET AND I'M TO
DECIDE WHEN TO RING THE FIRE BELL....
SERGEANT JONES'S ORDERS!"

"ANY COMPLAINTS?"
"NO SIR! VERY NICE SIR!"

a new Bar for the Mess out of boards and Jarrow taken from one of the bombed barrack blocks.

The WO wanted his pound of flesh. He wanted me on other jobs during the day, but provided I was prepared to start work at 17.00 he could pay me 2/6d an hour. He also pointed out that if I refused he would take my refusal personally. It was the sort of offer you couldn't refuse!

When I saw the lovely bar top (Jarrow is a rich red), I knew I could do a very good job – so starting with three grades of sandpaper, I worked from 17.00 to 22.00 hrs rubbing down. The second evening I spent applying Dragons Blood to give it the colour, on the third evening I rubbed down again with steel wool and flour paper. On the fourth evening I started polishing the top a little at a time.

It was coming up fine until two young Canadian Officers, chattering away like magpies and paying no attention, placed their hands in the moist and sticky polish in the area I was working on. I've never been one to stand on ceremony and I gave them a right telling off! I had to strip down and start again! Give them their due, a few minutes later one of the Mess Waiters appeared by my side with a couple of Scotches, compliments of the Canadian Officers. Free drinks, and Scotch at that, were hard to come by at any time. So I repaired the damage and pressed on.

In addition to the bar itself there were shelves and a lot of other woodwork that had to be French Polished. It looked as though I was going to be at it for quite a time and I hoped that they weren't in too much of a hurry, but here again I was going to have my plans changed!

After I'd been on the job for nearly a week, who should come to inspect progress but the Station Commander, Air Commodore Atcherley (who sadly was lost in the Suez affair). He said that he was well pleased and hoped I would be finished for the following weekend (which was the weekend of the Station Dance). I said I could do it, but it would mean working all my spare hours 'til the dance. (I didn't want to be tied down on the evening of the dance because I'd got a date with a WAAF from Signals.)

'I HOPE FOR YOUR SAKE, BOYO, THAT THE NEXT WORD IS SPLENDID'

WAS IT LIKE THIS FOR YOU?

Every night as I pushed on, a Scotch and chaser appeared at my side, compliments of Air Commodore Atcherley. As it happened I was working right up to the wire on the Saturday, and my WAAF and I had to meet at the Dance Bar later than planned. We were just about to order our first drink of the evening when we were intercepted by the Air Commodore and the Adjutant who invited us to the Officers Mess to inspect the new bar. He was delighted with the new bar, and my WAAF and I had all our drinks at the Station Dance on him!

But that was not all, Air Commodore Atcherley had decreed that there would be an Official Opening on the Sunday night with all the officers, myself, and the carpenters present. Glasses in hand, we watched as the name plate of the bar was unveiled:

THE COCK WELL INN

TILLET, HERTS

There was a roar of laughter as we read the sign, but I laughed twice as hard as everybody else. I was going to receive fifty hours overtime at 2/6d an hour . . . and being paid overtime in the Air Force was really something to laugh about! **Sid Arscott**

THE EYES AND EARS OF THE RAF   JANUARY 1949

Royal Air Force Station Dimlington was a Type 54 Coastal Radar Station just North of Spurn Point in East Yorkshire. Like all others of its kind it was perched on a cliff top overlooking the North Sea, with its underground Receiver Block with 150ft tower surmounted by a parabolic transmitter/ receiver.

Dimlington's role was two-fold, it had a range of 150,000 yards and could "see" up to 20,000ft, and was an early warning system against shipping and low flying aircraft. The station complement was some 35 bods, mainly Radar Operators, Mechanics and Fitters, plus an assortment of clerks, cooks, MT, a few SPs and a young Scottish F/Lt as CO.

At intervals, 73 Wing 90 Group would declare a station stand-down, but for the Type 54s only the Aircraft Watches were stood down. The shipping Watches had to be maintained, because most of the coastal minefields were still in place. In Dimlington's case part of its role was to ensure that shipping going into Hull stayed within the swept sea lanes, and if a ship appeared on the screens to be straying, then the Coastguards at Flamborough Head had to be informed so that they could warn the ship to steer away.

On one such stand-down one Radar Operator was highly choked that he'd drawn the role of night Shipping Watch. Since only one tube was used it meant that he would be on duty alone. He made his weary way along the coast from the Domestic Site to the Tech Site, entered the Ops Block, switched on, signed on the Station Log, and sat down in front of the set to watch the screen. His Log entries read as follows:-

22.00 *All Shipping proceeding safely outside Minefields.*
23.00   "   "   "   "

The log entries didn't vary until 03.00, but then his eyes started to get heavy...

At 04.20 the phone rang. Our hero picked it up, and an angry voice with a strong Yorkshire accent said, "Is that t'bloody RAF?"

"Yes," piped our hero, rubbing the sleepy dust from his eyes.

" 'Ave you seen anything on those magic tubes of your'n tonight?"

"No," replied our hero, envisaging Technical Charges galore. The maximum penalty for sleeping at your post was death by firing squad, and as a nineteen-year-old National Serviceman he could almost feel the blindfold being tied around his head!

"Well, go outside and 'ave a look you great daft girls blouse!"

The erk knew better than to argue with the Flamborough Coastguards and, burdened down with guilt, he put on his greatcoat, walked to the cliff edge and looked over.

Half-way down the 80' cliff he saw directly beneath him half a dozen fishermen climbing up towards him, and at the foot of the cliffs, on its side with the waves breaking over it, was a Hull trawler! Almost certainly it had been too close inshore to have been visible on the radar, but there was no point in taking any chances!

"THE EYES AND EARS OF THE AIR FORCE ... "

WAS IT LIKE THIS FOR YOU?

Without further ado, he rushed back to the Ops Block, took off the back of the radar set, and made some adjustments. Then he picked up the Station Log and made this entry:-

03.25. Set U/S. Am trying to locate fault.   *R. Suppards*

WHAT DID I DO ON D-DAY?

As the build-up to D-Day grew to a crescendo, the roads and rail became congested with sailors, soldiers and airmen moving towards what was to be one of Britain's greatest hours, and perhaps theirs too. But there was one airman who, with a small party of others, was travelling for- no reason at all so far as he could see.

It had all started with passing out from a trade course at Weeton, Near Blackpool, and being posted with a few others to an Airfield Construction Unit at Launceston in Cornwall. That journey had been enough to test the patience of a saint, but worse was to follow!

The Corporal who met us at the Railway Station told us to wait there whilst he made some arrangements for us.

"Where's the camp?" Someone asked.

"Ah," said the Corporal, "that's part of the problem, it's only a tent on the moors, with two occupants – myself and a Flight Lieutenant." (I was beginning to get a very nasty feeling about this Airfield Construction business.)

Anyhow the Corporal fixed us up with a meal at a local Fish and Chip Restaurant, and having put away sausages, tomatoes, mushrooms, eggs and two cups of tea, he told us to pick up our kit, and we were on the move again. This time marched to an American Camp where we were given an enormous hut at least 100 feet long and 40 feet wide, just for 12 of us. We spread ourselves out, and someone said, "We'll be really comfortable here!"

But this was not to be our new home! Oh no!

Next morning bright and early the Corporal and the Flight Looey told us to get back into marching order as we were on the move again. This time to Broad Clypt. Once more on the train going back the way we had come yesterday you could say we were getting just a teeny-weeny bit BRASSED OFF!

Broad Clypt turned out to be a USAF field full of Dakotas and Hadrian gliders with hundreds of Americans busily occupied in working on the aircraft, drilling, marching about and so on. The RAF presence on the airfield was restricted to one wooden office manned by a Sergeant and two erks.

"Where are our billets?" asked one.

He took us outside and pointed,

"Do you see that line of gliders?

"Yes, Sergeant."

"Then beyond that on the other side of the field do you see those Dakotas?"

"Yes, Sergeant".

"Well, beyond them can you see a hill?"

"Yes, Sergeant."

"Right, well your billets are on the far side of that hill!"

"Any transport, Sergeant?"

"No."

He then told us our duties were to fill in any holes on the airfield that prangs or enemy action might make – otherwise we had no duties. Every one was being very close-mouthed and we had no way of knowing that D-Day was now only three days away. As we stood disconsolately outside the hut wondering how to get across the airfield Lady Luck smiled on us. I recognized a US Army Sergeant I'd known on the course at Weeton. In no time he'd organized a 7 ton truck, our kit was loaded on it, he gave us cartons of cigarettes and candy bars, a pass to the PX for drinks and we ate like kings in their mess. We were confined to camp, and we knew something very Hush-hush was about to take place.

Flying went like clockwork on D-Day, no prangs, no enemy action. This was a great place to be we thought. The day after we were posted again! This time to Goodwood Park in Sussex.

So what did I do on D-Day? Well not a lot really!   *Sid Arscott*

WHAT THE WELL-DRESSED ERK WORE (C. 1946)

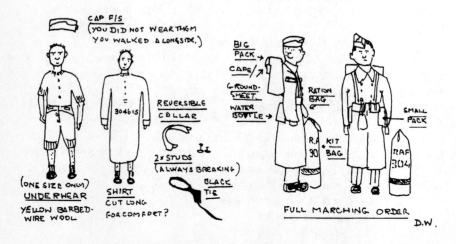

WAS IT LIKE THIS FOR YOU?

CHAPTER V

Service Overseas

Members of RAFA 310 have served in Royal Air Force establishments in every theatre of war and in most Post-War locations. To be a "proper" airman you had to achieve several distinctions. The marks of approval included, "getting your number dry", "getting some time in", and "getting your knees brown".

The following contributions by John Heath invoke memories of Service in the Middle East and Far East Commands, of troopships, khaki-drill, sand and bloodthirsty insects. The first contribution is about an anonymous airman who, though he doesn't say so, I strongly suspect is John himself!

The Advice Form which follows is humorous, but it has its poignant side too. The longer you were away, the harder it was to pick up the threads of civvy life.

HABBANIYA 1950

The Station Commander, driving along a Camp road, blue pennant flying, passes an airman who fails to salute him. Stopping his vehicle, the Station Commander calls the negligent airman back.

"Why did you not salute me?" he asked.

"Sorry, Sir," the airman replied smartly, "but I didn't see you!"

"What is your Unit?"

"Bahrain, Sir."

"Well, why are you here?"

"To attend a Specialist Appointment at the Hospital, Sir!"

"Would that be to see the Optician?"

"Yes Sir!"

Exit Station Commander with nothing more to say in a cloud of dust, and exit airman in opposite direction, grinning.   ***John Heath***

"STAND STILL! I'LL TELL YOU WHEN TO MOVE!"

From:-Moral Welfare Branch.
HQ. MIDDLE EAST COMMAND

TO.................. (PARENT OR NEXT OF KIN/RELATIVE/FRIEND)

You are hereby notified of the return of the undermentioned to the United Kingdom:

No........... Rank.......................... Name...

Unit.. Address..

Date of Departure...................... By Sea/Air. Reason for Return...........................

This man will be shortly in your midst again, dehydrated and demoralised, to take his place in the community once more. You are therefore advised to observe carefully the following instructions, as necessary, taking into account, and making adequate allowance for the environment to which he has been subjected for the past 12/24 months.

(A) Lock any female contacts you have in the cellar or attic or get rid of them entirely if between the ages of nine and ninety.

(B) Fill fridge with beer. Remember he will only drink it cold, straight from the can or bottle.

(C) When serving rarities such as bread and butter, milk or fancy cakes, do not be alarmed if he goes at the food like a wild animal with cries of, *taman mungarea* (Arabic for good food). There is a marked tendency for personnel who have served up-country in the Radfan area to snatch their food and retreat to a corner, where they will squat and gloat over the food before devouring it in great gulps.

(D) When he arrives at the station ensure he is met with a guide. If on his arrival he greets you with *"kiff harlak"*, do not be alarmed, this only means "how are you". To make him feel more at home, it will be helpful to reply *"tamam"* meaning "very well."

(E) on boarding a bus buy his ticket for him. This will prevent the inevitable argument with the conductor as he bargains for a lower fare. This also applies when shopping. He is accustomed to paying what he feels is the true value of an article and NOT what he is asked for it. Failure to observe this precaution can result in disastrous consequences.

(F) if on passing the following objects he seems surprised or frightened, reassure him gently and explain what they are: Double-decker bus, trees, grass, train, youth with long hair, policeman, fish and chip shop, and possibly, most importantly a Public House.

PLEASE SEE OVER

WAS IT LIKE THIS FOR YOU?

From Moral Welfare Branch *continued*

(G) IF HE SHOULD DO ANY OF THE FOLLOWING PLEASE REFRAIN FROM CALLING A PSYCHIATRIST. REMEMBER HE HAS BEEN IN ADEN TOO LONG!

1. Sits on the floor cross-legged for long periods.

2. Walks around wearing only a towel.

3. Pours gravy on his sweet and mixes peaches with his mashed spuds.

4. If on waking first thing in the morning he screams, "Chico!" (Small Arab boy who is his bearer) "...*chai!*" (tea), the best treatment is to dress the smallest member of the family in a coloured skirt and a very dirty shirt, smear his/her face and hands with brown boot polish and get him/her to run to his bedside with a cup of tea.

N.B. This tea should have stewed for at least one hour and MUST be only luke-warm. (A pot of tea left over from the previous day and re-heated is ideal for this purpose.)

5. Be tolerant and understanding if he should answer the telephone with "*sayeda*" and finish with "*ma salaam*" (Arabic for hello and goodbye)

(a) NEVER mention any of the following within his hearing:

Sand, Lovely Summers day, Trips to the Seaside, Aden, Nasser or Mr. Wilson!

(b) It might prove advisable to obtain an Anglo/Arabic dictionary as this will prove valuable in securing a quicker and closer understanding with each other.

Finally, please bear in mind that beneath that dirty sun-tanned skin there beats a heart of gold. Treat him with kindness, understanding and an occasional pint of good beer, and you will soon see a likeness to the human being you once knew.

SIGNED .... (PADRE)

TWICE-ARMED IS TWICE ARMED   LAHORE 1943

My RSU was on the move up into Burma. The RAF Medical Branch, at the last minute decided they wanted to have another go at turning us into pin cushions with a last-minute jab for cholera.

The building that the medics had chosen to do the deed consisted of a very long corridor in which we queued leading into a fair-sized room where the MO and his assistants waited, armed with innumerable hypodermics and pints of vaccine.

As I drew closer to the place of execution I could see that there was a continuing corridor beyond where the MO and his Henchmen were. At the end of that corridor was an Indian Air Force MO with his band of helpers giving each airman as he passed another jab in the left arm.

The MO told me to roll up my left sleeve. Now I'm left-handed so I asked the MO if I could please have BOTH jabs in my right arm.

"What do you mean both jabs?" he asked irritably.

"Well Sir, there's an Indian Doctor giving everybody a second jab as they pass him."

He looked in the direction I indicated.

"The silly bugger!" he exploded, "he's here to help us cope with the numbers.... you only need ONE jab for cholera!" He grinned, "Still, the lot that have already gone through will be 200% proof against it!"

Bernard Dee

THE RHINE AND THE RHONE   RAF SUTTON BRIDGE, SUMMER 1947

At this time, Sutton Bridge was HQ 73 Wing 90 Group. Also known as Northern Signals Area. One of its responsibilities was staffing the 60 or so Radar Stations that covered the Northern British Isles. With demob going on apace it was probably somewhat of an administrative nightmare manning these small units which could be Chain Home, Chain Home (Low), Chain Home (Extra Low), GEE, GCI and Mobile Radar Units, with appropriately trained Radar Fitters, Mechs and Operators. Even more because some stations were exclusively WAAF and others exclusively RAF.

After the Invasion of 1944 two chains of Mobile Radar Units were established. The Rhine Chain exclusively RAF and the Rhone Chain exclusively WAAF, both of which came under the administrative control of Sutton Bridge.

I was at Sutton Bridge waiting posting. What administrative genius decided to close both the Rhine and Rhone Chains at the same time I shall never discover. The airmen and Waafs had each been overseas for a couple of years, and some 150 of each arrived at Sutton Bridge within a day or two of each other to await postings.

Well, by the end of the week they'd all paired off two and two. The normal activity practised in the back row of the village cinema (hand-holding and snogging) extended right down to the front row. Looking back one has to remember how young we all were – most of us not old enough to vote.

Within a fortnight DROs carried the instruction "Airmen and WAAFs are not to be found in compromising positions on the perimeter track."

In six weeks from the closure of the Rhine and Rhone Chains we'd all been posted to outstations...

But what a five weeks it was!   *R. Suppards*

PLUS CA CHANGE   DUM-DUM AIRPORT CALCUTTA 1945

After the end of the War with Japan the glider unit I was on was disbanded and I was posted as a Sergeant Fitter IIa to Royal Air Force Station Dum-Dum Calcutta (Air Force Station and Trading Post).

I found myself in charge of Night-Flying Servicing for the Squadron's Dakotas, visiting aircraft and sundry back-up services. Included in my charges were three De Haviland Rapides (Service name Dominies – twin-engined biplanes) exclusively used by the Governor of Bengal (plus pith helmet!) and his Staff.

Protocol demanded that His Excellency took off first, followed by the other two aircraft carrying the lower ranking entourage and his body guard.

"YOU DIDN'T JOIN THE AIR FORCE TO LOOK AT AIRCRAFT! EYES FRONT!"

On landing the Governor's aircraft landed last, so that there was always a ready-made Guard of Honour waiting for him on the Tarmac.

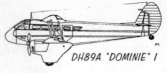

DH89A 'DOMINIE' I

The new Labour Government rewarded its supporters munificently, and Fred Burrows, Leader of the Railwaymen's' Union was knighted and made the new Governor of Bengal.

In his inaugural speech he said, and I quote, "Most of my predecessors have been accustomed to "huntin' and Shootin' whilst my life has been spent hootin' and Shuntin' ".

However, there was no change to the protocol!

Hugh Oxley

SMALL WORLD!

On 26th November 1955 I embarked in the troopship *Empire Orwell* on becoming Tourex (Tour Expired) in Hong-Kong. Already on board were troops returning home from Korea.

One day on deck I got into conversation with a Military Policeman who told me he was from Birmingham. On learning that I lived in Leamington he said, "Do you know the Queens Head Public House?"

"Yes," I replied, "its on the Canal bridge!"

He then told me that he'd never been there, but his parents had just taken over the licence. He then asked me if I could call on them and tell them he and his family would be coming to see them on Boxing Day (we docked at Southampton on December 22nd).

This I did.

At the end of my disembarkation leave I was posted to Headquarters, Home Command at White Waltham.

Although the location of the Unit was very nice, unfortunately the Section I was employed in was not, so I made discreet enquiries as to how I might get a move into the Midlands. I was advised that a Sergeant Freeman Fox in the Command Drafting Office might be able to help me.

On locating the said SNCO, I asked what my chances were.

"Where do you live?" he asked.

"Leamington Spa." I replied.

To my amazement he then asked,

"Do you know the Queens Head pub?"

I replied that I did.

"My Brother-in-Law keeps it," he said, and then he asked, "How would you like to go to Cosford Hospital?"

Three days later I was on my way!

John Heath

'IF YOU'RE GOING TO ADVANCE LIKE THAT, PUT YOUR HELMET ON YOUR ARSE!'

THE LANGUAGE BARRIER   USA 1943

As the Empire Flying Training Scheme got under way more and more RAF ground-crew were required in Canada to support the efforts of the flying schools. They were places in the "sticks" with names like Red Deer, Moose Jaw, Penhold, Gimli and the like. I was shipped out from Liverpool in 1943 with hundreds of others on the *Louis Pasteur* bound in the first instance for New York. In 1943 the U-Boat menace was very real, and when we broke down in Mid-Atlantic, two days out of New York, everybody was wondering, if worst came to worst, we could swim that far! After five very long hours we got going again and we all recommenced breathing.

Disembarking in New York we were ferried to New England and then by train to Taunton, Massachusetts, arriving the following morning. There we were marched to an Assembly Hall where an American Major addressed us. He told us we would be held here for a few days before going off to our various Flying Schools. He welcomed us to America and in his speech advised us of the Rules of Security. He said we could each send a telegram home – but to keep it brief – he recommended *"Arrived US."*

Howls of laughter greeted this. Knackered after our journey we might be... U/S we were *not*! It took one of our officers to explain what we were laughing about – at that time the Americans did not use "U/S" to mean "unserviceable".   ***Gordon Powis***

WAS IT LIKE THIS FOR YOU?

INNOCENTS ABROAD

In the early fifties a party of a dozen P/Os crossed the Atlantic for training in Canada. The officer i/c draft was an F/O (ex-Cranwell) called Hugh. The ship was small, the weather was atrocious. The Captain said it was the worst storm conditions he'd encountered in 25 years.

We were four to a cabin and we didn't see our stewards from the time we left Liverpool until we arrived at Halifax, Nova Scotia – they'd been seasick the whole time! It was a case of fending for yourself.

We stayed on our feet by permanently occupying the bar, playing "Black Queen" and taking frequent doses of stabilizing alcohol. On that voyage we made an important discovery. If one maintained the level of alcohol in the bloodstream at a reasonably high level the compensating physical mechanism which served to keep you upright when "stoned" served also to act as a trimming device to help you to keep your sea-legs; and so we avoided seasickness. The crossing took four days longer than advertised due to the bad weather, and the bar was running out of alcohol.

Hugh was getting concerned about the fact that he and his charges were going to arrive at RCAF London Ontario as confirmed alcoholics, so on docking at Halifax he insisted that we all went ashore, got our land-legs, and started the weaning process.

'I TOLD YOU NOT TO USE 100 OCTANE IN YOUR LIGHTER!'

As we stepped ashore panic hit us. We'd become so accustomed to living in a world of constant movement that Halifax seemed to be pitching and rolling worse than the *S.S. Newfoundland* had done.

"What we need to do," announced Hugh, "is to find a restaurant, sit down, and get some food into us."

The first identifiable building we saw was an enormous Dickensian institution entitled "Orphanage". Then as the "fearless aviators" clinging to each other for mutual support staggered past the orphanage we spied next door – a restaurant! Owlishly we crowded round the menu in the window and focused with difficulty on the small print. Heading the list was:-

TONITE'S SPECIAL – Braised Ribs of Baby

We stared at it.

"Great God!" exclaimed Hugh "they must get the babies from the orphanage next door! We didn't practice cannibalism at Cranwell and I don't intend to start it now!"

It was a day or two later before we discovered that Canadians weren't cannibals, and that the *baby* referred to meant *calf*!

R. Suppards

WOT?-NO SHOWER?   DUM-DUM AIRPORT 1946

Signal received by Control Tower RAF Dum-Dum 20.00 hrs.

Lord Louis Mountbatten Supreme Commander Allied Forces South East Asia Command arr. 21.00. Three aircraft.
1. Flying Ops. Signals Control Centre.
2. Supreme Commander's Staff.
3. Supreme Commander, Senior Officers and attendants.

A Guard of Honour was rapidly laid on, and then the party swept away to the Governor's residence. Overnight the 3 aircraft were serviced for a scheduled take-off at 09.00hrs.

WOT – NO SHOWER ?

08.45hrs. Station Commander phones from Control tower to Flight Dispersal Point.

"Group Captain Slee speaking, everything ready for take-off Sergeant?"

"Er, Yessir ... except..."

"Except what?"

"Waiting for the water bowser, Sir!"

"What's that for, Sergeant?"

"To fill the water tank for The Supremo's shower. Sir!"

"Never mind that Sergeant, cancel it – he'll have to manage without! He MUST fly out on time!"

"Very Good, Sir!"

I have often wondered whether the Supremo uttered those immortal words of CHAD when he stripped, stepped into the shower, pulled the operating chain ... and nothing happened!

Hugh Oxley

WHODUNNIT?

I passed out from Cosford as a Flight Mech, arriving at No.1 PDC on April 1st 1943. Two days later we were off to Morecambe to be issued with our Tropical kit. The kit issue was being made from two Big Stores, one of which was Littlewoods.

We were "fell in" at the back of the Stores on a big patch of open ground to wait. At the far end of the open area a fairground roundabout was being erected for the Spring/Summer Season. It was the only thing of interest around us as we stood static. People became restless because, like every kit issue, nothing was happening. Other luckless bods who had stood there "all hope abandoned" had written desolate messages on the wall like "Died Waiting" with their name and date. Yet still we stood like dumb patient oxen.

Some of the lads decided they might just as well rest their tired feet on the roundabout and went over to sit on it. Others followed, and in seconds the roundabout was a mass of blue-uniformed erks piled on it revolving at a tremendous rate of knots!

Suddenly there was an almighty crash, and the roundabout disintegrated in a cloud of dust!

In a flash there was not a single body anywhere NEAR the wreckage. Thereafter, when one squad passed another, one squad would call out, "Who broke the roundabout?" and the other would respond with a chorus of, "The Merry-go round broke down!" On the troopship the same joke was played, and when in the convoy one trooper passed close to another, the challenge and the delighted response passed from ship to ship across the intervening sea. This was an evergreen joke at Beer Nights, Christmas Dinners and the like, until postings away caused it to die out.

In June 1993 I was at lunch at Scampton during a Reunion of the RSUs of Assam and Burma, and a stranger sat at my table. I found out he'd done almost the same trip as me on the *Aorangi* from Cosford–Morecambe–Bombay–Quetta then later to Agatala. I asked, "Who broke the roundabout?" He nearly fell off his chair! I was the first bloke he'd met since who remembered that day at Morecambe. I really made his day!   ***Bernard Dee***

IT REALLY DOES BAFFLE BRAINS   RAF WITTERING, 1952

The Wing Commander Flying was a very keen golfer and a dedicated competitor. When a rather important match was lost on very suspicious recorded scores by the opposition, his diplomacy was taken to the limit, and to great applause from his team he stated that "as far as he knew, there were no snakes on the course, but there were certainly a few bad adders!"

The squadron commander had been on a man management course, and came back full of ideas on participation, consultation, empowerment and large dollops of Maslow and Herzberg.

When we went on detachment in the Middle East it provided him with a wonderful opportunity to practise his new found theories.

Our first meeting was to decide on the layout of the eating/mess areas. He announced that on this detachment we would all eat together or apart, depending on the consensus of opinion. Surprisingly, it was decided that the technicians, the training staff and the senior officers should have separate areas. To enable easy identification of the areas another meeting was called to decide on suitable names for each area. After much discussion the names were decided, based on English Counties. This caused the squadron commander much embarrassment because although he could accept the Worcester room, abbreviated to Worcs for the workers, the Staffordshire room, abbreviated to Staffs for the staff, he refused to accept the Berkshire room for the senior officers!

He did learn, however, that theory and practise are sometimes very awkward bedfellows!   *Arthur Walton*

CONCEALED WEAPON?   DUM-DUM AIRPORT 1946

Dum-Dum was a staging post for aircraft making refuelling stop-overs going East or West. One evening at 20.00 hours we recieved this signal:-

"Expect York aircraft arriving 21.00 hours carrying Crown Prince Phumibol (Son of the Golden Umbrella) heir to The Imperial Throne of Siam (Thailand) for refuelling and overnight stopover en route to Bangkok for Coronation." (The Crown Prince had been smuggled out of Siam just before it fell to Japan in order to complete his education in Switzerland.)

At 21.00 the York landed and a small group of diminutive Siamese VIPs, all in charcoal grey suits, together with their escorts, were whisked away to the Governor's Residence.

At 23:00, Panic Stations! The RAF Police arrived in a muck sweat to search the York. The Sword of State was missing!

Finding no trace of it on the aircraft the RAF Police lined the whole ground-crew, myself included, for a body search, looking for a concealed weapon. As explanation we were told that the Crown Prince couldn't continue his journey until The Sword of State was found as it was an integral part of the Coronation Ceremony's Regalia.

Forty eight hours later it turned up in Karachi where it had been left behind at the previous stop-over. It was flown post-haste to Dum-Dum, and the Crown Prince carried it aboard the York himself. It was at least five feet long, and how the RAFPs could conceive that it could be concealed about the person I shall never fathom!   *Hugh Oxley*

WHY ARE WE ALL SO BLOODY-MINDED?   WINNIPEG 1955

When Scandinavian Air Services opened their route from Stockholm to Winnipeg flying over the Pole in a Constellation, the hype that attended the arrival of the first flight was nauseatingly "over the top" if you will excuse the pun! The reception SAS got was comparable to the reception the natives gave Columbus when he discovered America!

The RAF and RCAF aircrews had been flying their DC3s and 4s up to the top of the World for years. They used a system called 'Grid Gyro Grivation' which substituted for the fact that the Compass was useless in high latitudes due to the proximity of the Magnetic North Pole. It required two navigators both working their ducks off, one plotting and the other constantly taking Astro observations.

What SAS had to help them was the new Kollsmann Periscopic Sextant which took most of the sweat out of the Astro work, which of course we did not have.

When those tall blond Swedes stepped out of their "Connie" they were wearing dark blue uniforms and immaculate white shirts. They looked as though they'd stepped out of a band-box. We wore Canadian issue flying kit known as "goon-skins" and even *looked* smelly when we finished a trip. Somehow we felt offended and when their arrival was shown at the cinema in the News reels we were, frankly, jealous.

How we chortled when we heard that the next flight landed at Edmonton, about 400 miles West of Winnipeg, due to mis-operation of their posh new Sextant. Of course *that* didn't get on the Newsreels.

It was the same year that the first Vickers Viscount was delivered to Winnipeg, in I think, Trans-Canada livery. Everyone, RCAF, RAF and the Civil lines that shared the airfield were interested in it. It was a pretty aircraft, standing poised for flight in the sunlight... just perfect!

Then a party of very Senior officers came across from Ottawa to "evaluate" it. On the day after it had arrived it was a sad broken thing. Nobody knew who'd flown it into the deck, nobody had been hurt, but we were pretty certain the pilot had been of Air rank. It's a sad comment on human nature but the junior officers, when they heard about it, needed to put on dry underwear...   *R. Suppards*

A GERMAN LESSON?

In the Summer of 1958 I was stationed at Gutersloh, and the SWO was the terror of the junior officers. I was a pretty senior F/O, but I still didn't feel safe when anywhere near him. He was brisk, immaculately uniformed, bull-mad, an ex-Brat and a Yorkshireman. If that wasn't enough, he'd never been known to say please or thank you, and was an obsequious crawler round Squadron Leaders and above.

I had a duty trip to do one day and the SAC driver (who was a chatty lad) and I fell into swapping anecdotes about the SWO. Strictly *infra-dig* I know, but as far as he was concerned I had no conscience. The driver told me that one day he had to take the SWO on a long trip and was suffering badly from the SWO's back-seat driving when suddenly he said,

"Driver, stop here!"

"What's the matter, Sir?" asked the Driver.

"We're somewhere near the Mohne Dam and I want to see it. Ask that German over there wearing the *lederhosen* and the funny green hat for directions!"

"But I don't speak German," said the SAC.

"I'll make him understand," declared the SWO.

He rolled down the car window and barked, *"Kommen-Sie hier!"*

The German came slowly to the car.

"Wo ist der Mohne Dam?" the SWO said enunciating as though speaking to an idiot.

The German poked his head into the window and said in very good English. "English Air Force?"

"Of course! growled the SWO.

"Well," said the German, *"Bitte* is the word for please, and if your pilots could find it in the War when we were shooting at them, I suggest you do the same thing they did... bloody well look for it!"

With that he turned on his heel and walked away.

The driver said the SWO didn't say another word on the way back but "By bloody 'ell the Germans are a rude bloody lot!"

Recounted by an Anonymous ex-F/Lt Canberra Pilot

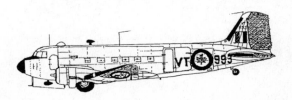

"IF AT ANY TIME YOU GIRLS FEEL YOU ARE ABOUT TO DISGRACE
THE ROYAL AIR FORCE UNIFORM YOU WEAR... TAKE IT OFF!"

"NOW DON'T FORGET, IF IT DOESN'T OPEN... BRING IT BACK!"

WAS IT LIKE THIS FOR YOU?

CHAPTER VI

Memories of the WAAF

The WAAFs served on a Station as R/T Ops, W/Ops, Parachute Packers, Cooks, MT Drivers, Pay accounts and countless other trades. It was noticeable that when there were WAAFs around how language improved. Airmen in their presence almost strangled themselves in the effort not to use the REALLY naughty words. The R/T Ops who were in contact with aircraft in Flying Control would often hear aircrew venting their feelings in words that were not found in most dictionaries. It was part of the duties of these operators to log verbatim all messages, and with a perfectly straight face these girls would meticulously log every word. They sometimes made spelling errors – but you never saw a log with the naughty words mis-spelt. I just hope they didn't know what they meant!

They lived in the *Waffery* where they were guarded by WAAF NCOs known as 'dragons'. It must have been difficult for them, for the WAAFs were masters of the art of evasion if they had a date they wanted to keep. Nobody, male or female, was allowed off the station after 23.59 whilst under the age of 21 – but the WAAFs knew more ways of getting on and off camp, avoiding the Main Gate, than most Airmen did. The Dragons' job must have been like trying to catch smoke!

"NO SIR! MY BALLOONS ARE NOT OVER-INFLATED!"

All WAAFs seemed to wear the same perfume, 'Californian Poppy'. In fact if you were sitting in a cinema and you suddenly smelt Californian Poppy you knew there was a WAAF somewhere near.

Another of their attributes was their enormously efficient jungle telegraph. Typically, a WAAF in Flying Control might casually ask you the name of that new Radar Fitter on GCA. Once you'd given her his name, she would want to know where he came from, how old he was and had he got a girlfriend etc. If you then asked her if she was 'interested' in him she would say (usually truthfully) "No, but Mary in Pay Accounts had seen him in the Airman's Mess yesterday and thought he was smashing!"

The next time the Radar Fitter was in the NAAFI one of the Parachute Packers would start to chat to him. After a few minutes she would introduce Mary as her friend. So Mary had been introduced properly and didn't look 'forward'. WAAFs? They were as artful as a waggon load of monkeys!

HARDLY CONFUSED AT ALL!   WADDINGTON SPRING 1948

Minnie was an 18 year old ACW2 R/T Operator on the Morning Watch on Flying Control. There was a lot of air traffic that morning: our three squadrons of Lincolns were airborne; Avro, who shared the airfield with us, were testing some converted Ansons; the OCU was flying its Mosquitos and the USAF were operating a couple of busy squadrons of light aircraft – all from the same field.

Air Traffic discipline was good, except for the Americans who scorned our 'Limey' routines. Often, the first thing an R/T Operator would hear would be an American voice saying, *"Expeditor four seven landing on two-six"* – and there the plane would be, already taxiing down the runway! Never mind that the R/T Op might be holding 3 Lincolns in circuit, with another on 'finals' and a Mosquito with undercart and flaps down as Number two to land!

Pacemaker Baker (a Lincoln) had just called up for landing instructions, and Minnie was giving the pilot the runway in use, altimeter setting, wind direction and a circuit height of 1,000 feet, when a strong Texan voice broke into her transmission with, *"Buckmaster Fox coming in on Two-Six"*

Flustered, Minnie replied, "Buckmaster Fox you are NOT clear to land, maintain circuit at 1,000 feet, you are number FIVE to land"... but clapped her hand to her mouth stricken with horror as she heard herself transpose the B and the F of the Buckmaster's Call-sign (Minnie was a well brought-up young woman who NEVER used the F-word!).

The American pilot's laugh floated through the ether as he touched down...
"Sorry Babe!"

Fury added to fluster, as she tried to log the American's conversation with one hand and simultaneously direct Pacemaker Baker. Now hopelessly flustered she pushed her mike button and said, "Basemaker Paker hold circuit at ten thousand feet" (meaning to say ONE thousand feet).

An aggrieved pilot replied, *"Tower from Pacemaker Baker... It'll take us all day to get up to ten thousand feet. Suggest you make the Yank aircraft with the rude call-sign do circuits all day and let us good boys land now!"*

That was it... poor Minnie burst into tears.

R. Suppards

The A/PO was Nobody's Friend!

"GENTLEMEN! I'D ADVISE YOUR PARENTS TO 'AVE YOU PUT DOWN AND TRY AGAIN!"

"WHERE DID YOU GET YOUR WINGS?"
"MOSS BROS, SIR!"

"THE SQDN LDR SAID YOU WERN'T FIT TO PILOT A WHEELBARROW!"

"BUT I DEFENDED YOU ..."

"... I SAID YOU WERE!"

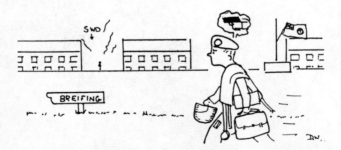

"MR FOTHERINGAY-BROWN, YOUR RIGHT SHOELACE IS UNDONE!"

WAS IT LIKE THIS FOR YOU?

CHAPTER VII

ACSB and Beyond

Entry into Air Crew started with ACSB. Most people called it Air Crew Selection Board – but its proper name was Aviation Candidates Selection Board. (Probably to please the Americans – like calling 68 Fighter Squadron the 68th Pursuit!)

Here you spent somewhere between a week and a fortnight undergoing Aptitude Tests and a Medical Board. All the Tests were a little daunting, but "blowing up the mercury" was the one that *really* made your eyes water! A column of mercury in a glass tube had to be blown up via a tube and mouthpiece and held above a red mark. To help you there was also a clip on your nose.

After what seemed hours, but was less than a minute you were told, "OK, stop". By this time you were so close to expiring it didn't seem to matter if you stopped or not! Following the last of the tests you were led into the final board where a group of officers with rings up to their armpits and medal ribbons down to their waist sat behind a table and glared at you. One by one they asked questions and all went fairly well with 17-year-old R. Suppards until one of the gilded Mighty Ones asked why he wanted to become a member of Air Crew. "I want to fly," said Our Hero.

The Senior Officer with a face like an angry bull slammed the table with the flat of his hand and roared, "No you don't, you want to use an aircraft as a weapon against the Countries Enemies!" R. Suppards jumped so high he solo'd without the aid of an aircraft! He'd never quite looked at air-warfare that way before!

In case anybody thinks that Air Crew training was about carrying out duties *in the air*, this was only partly true! There were courses on Engines: nasty dirty things! And if one packs up in the air, who's going to get out on the wing to fix it? Theory of Flight: either the thing will stay in the air or it won't!

Manual of Air Force Law: zzzzzzzzzzz!

Statics and Dynamics: Forces on an aircraft in dive and bank. Don't we trust the designers then?

'GET THE FEEL FOR THE AIRCRAFT... STIR THE STICK PUDDING-WISE!'

Hygiene: well if I don't know enough to keep myself clean by now, I shouldn't be here!

Physical Training: long runs, swimming, games. Very wearisome!

Service Etiquette: all about wearing proper headdress when in mufti, leaving appropriate visiting cards and writing Service letters.

Gradually the secret thought that perhaps the Air Force didn't have any aeroplanes was dispelled, and hours started to appear in the log-book. Subjects like Met, Navigation, Signals, Map reading, Astro, Cross Countries etc. were introduced. Since all subjects were examination subjects whether in the air or on the ground, there were Handling Checks, Phase Checks and Progress Checks, and every one had to be passed. That meant lots of SWOTTING! Every mark counted, but one of the Finals Questions in Air Safety to u/t Navigators was, "What is the Chief cause of panic in the air?" This was a multi-choice question, of which the choices were:

'A MONKEY COULD MAKE A BETTER LANDING THAN THIS!'

(A) Shortage of Fuel? (B) Enemy Action? (C) The Pilot? (D) Adverse Weather? (E) Fire?

Although many were struggling for marks not one could resist choosing (C) – although the correct answer was (E)!

Eventually came Wings Parade, and after a short leave, more training and more progress tests. By then you had completely forgotten that you had joined the Air Force to fly, and had learned that flying was a VERY serious business, in which mistakes were often fatal! Despite this, nearly all aircrew have a touch of P/O Prune in their system somewhere. On the following pages there are incidents of Prunisms which all happened, not necessarily to R. Suppards – but he knew some one who did!

A LESSON IN SERVICE ETIQUETTE   RAF KIRTON IN LINDSAY

In the early fifties, Kirton in Lindsay was the ITS for pilots and navigators. At the end of the course the vast majority were commissioned as Acting Pilot Officers, and before being posted to Flying Training Units were required to spend a fortnight living in the Officers Mess at KL. During the training considerable emphasis was laid on Service Etiquette. Since most people had only joined because they wanted to fly, becoming an officer, and by implication a gentleman, was an added complication. A/POs had been conditioned to be very wary of such details as what headgear an officer should wear in mufti, and how to walk when carrying a rolled umbrella. Instructions as to behaviour were complicated. For example, "Officers, when in mufti, on hearing the National Anthem will remove their headgear and stand to Attention. If alone and in uniform the officer will salute, if in company with other officers the senior officer present will salute and the junior officers will stand at attention. Just before 23.00 the radio was switched on in the ante-room to pick up the News. There were officers in uniform, others in mufti seated comfortably in green leather armchairs, and six A/POs sitting on hard chairs huddled together for protection at the far end of the ante-room. As the News finished came the National Anthem. Peter and John leapt to attention, Mike was making violent hand signals to tell them to sit down. Bill assumed the "crouch", so that to those he felt wanted him to stand, and those who he wanted to convince that he was sitting could be equally persuaded. None of the seated officers made a move and continued to read their newspapers. Derek stood up to express solidarity with Peter and John just as Peter sat down and Allan decided to stand. An elderly Squadron Leader rustled his newspaper and glared over his spectacles at us. We all sat down, our frail self-confidence severely dented.

'I SAID LOSE 500FT OF ALTITUDE. THIS ISN'T A BLOODY STUKA!'

Over breakfast the following morning we decided that we had learned two things. 1. Officers do not stand to attention in the Mess for the Anthem. 2. Most importantly they do not BOB UP AND DOWN to the National Anthem!

R. Suppards

DRINK CANADA DRY!
RAF PRESTWICK – RCAF GOOSE BAY
1952

'THAT WAS NOT A LANDING. THE BEST YOU COULD CALL IT WAS A CONTROLLED CRASH!'

In the early fifties the RCAF used to frequently fly their North Stars (which were DC4s with Rolls-Royce engines) back and forth between the East Coast of Canada and Prestwick in Scotland. To do this, if you've got the fuel you can fly

"HEY NAV, WHERE ARE WE?"
"SORRY I CAN'T SAY, I'VE LOST MY PENCIL!"

straight along the appropriate Line of Latitude, or you can fly a Great Circle route. The Great Circle route describes a curve on the plotting chart, requiring regular alterations of course – its a lot of work for the navigator but it saves several hundred miles, and it allowed the North Stars to complete the crossing with some fuel in their tanks rather than just the smell. A certain RCAF Navigator always looked forward to his trips to Scotland because he enjoyed sampling the limitless varieties of Scotch available. Normally there was at least 24 hours lay-over so that he would be able to clear his head before it was time to get into the air again. But, there's a rock in every snowball, and one night Mac had hardly got to bed before he was warned for briefing in an hour as his flight had been brought forward. Feeling like death he worked out his Flight Plan, drew his required tracks on his Mercator, and floated out to his aircraft.

Once out over the Atlantic he picked up his sextant, planning to take a 3-Star fix. Carelessly he put his hand onto what he falsely thought was the "steady" handle only to realize too late that in fact he had pulled the emergency release which jettisoned the Astro-dome. He only just managed to prevent himself from being sucked out into the black Atlantic night but was unable to prevent all his instruments, charts and tables

" PHEW!"

NAVIGATOR'S LOG... "3-STAR FIX THAT PUT US OVER MOSCOW DISCARDED. ETA THORNEY ISLAND 6 MINUTES!"

flying past him and out into the night. Now "Mac", was a resourceful chap (and by now completely sober!), so he reviewed his options. He came to a decision. If he could fabricate a chart he would press on. But all his maps had gone, and he knew the pilot hadn't got any. Then he remembered the pilot always liked to bring a few bottles of Canada Dry aboard, and suddenly he saw in his mind's eye the Canada Dry Label. It was a chart of the Atlantic and the East Canadian coast. Borrowing the pilots pencil, and an empty bottle of Canada Dry (after "Mac's performance with the Astro-dome the pilot wouldn't trust him with a full one) he set to work using the Canada Dry label as a model to draw an enlarged version on his Nav table.

Ten hours later, and almost exactly on ETA, they hit Goose Bay right on the nose, the only aircraft to have ever navigated the Atlantic with the aid of a soft-drink's label!

From that day onwards (so the story goes), Mac always carried a bottle of Canada Dry in his Nav Bag.

WAS IT LIKE THIS FOR YOU?

AS IT HAPPENED. . .

The year was 1943, and I was one of three Fitter IIa's stationed at RAF Longtown near Gretna Green – a quiet satellite drome operating Beaufighters. Suddenly all eyes were drawn skywards as a stranger "Maggie" started on its approach to our field. There was a wind blowing across the field gusting to gale force, and the "Maggie" appeared to be attempting to land away from the runways on the grass. Suddenly a gust blew the aircraft onto its back, too late for the pilot to recover!

We were rooted to the spot, watching and waiting for the inevitable to happen. It did, and we sprinted across the turf to give assistance. There was no fire, thank God!

Our shouts of, "Are you alright, gentlemen?" brought a response from the senior airman who reaching into a top tunic pocket exclaimed,

"No dammit, I've broken my pipe!"

Roy Rowberry

'YES, MARS IS RED... BUT YOU'VE JUST TAKEN A SIGHT ON THE PORT NAVIGATION LIGHT!'

FORGOTTEN ANYTHING?

Three hundred miles north-west of Winnipeg nearly forty years ago there was nothing. Lakes, forests giving way to Tundra – that was all. It was tranquil in our Dakota. The Radio Compass was working well, there was a full moon, making Astro observations easy, the wind was pretty constant, making the airplot look nice and tidy, and the moonlight on the snow filled me with a sense of wellbeing. Then Shoemaker F/O RCAF upset all that. The intercom sputtered and he said, "Hey Nav, we've got engine trouble, give me our position, I want to put out a "Securité".

This was the lowest level of Distress Call, the next level up was "Pan", and imminent "falling out of the sky, was "Mayday". I gave him the Lat and Long of our DR position and then plotted a course to our nearest diversion which was 150 nautical miles away, and in a Dak that was an hour's flying time. I then went up to the office to show him the topo chart.

"I don't understand this," he said, "I'm losing revs in both engines. I think I'd better put out a *Pan*."

AIRBORNE INTERCEPTION TRAINING.... "ONE, THEY'RE ON OUR SIDE! TWO, IF THEY WEREN'T WE'D FIRE AT THEM NOT BLOODY RAM THEM"

CRIKEY!

@!!!*

CLOSING SPEED 1200 KNOTS

He did that over the R/T and I went back to put out the same message on the W/T. We weren't flying with a W/Op that night just the pilot and myself. He turned onto the diversion course I'd plotted, and I went back to my seat to get another fix. Half my mind was on the drills to follow if we had to jump. The normal rule was that in those conditions you attempted to stay with the aircraft – but anything could happen from now on. It was 40° below zero on the ground. Then he said,

"I'm making it a *Mayday*!"

I gave him our new position, and Started the Crash Drill. Put Nav kit in Nav Bag, undo Pilot's safety harness and ensure his parachute was properly fastened. Lift and bring inboard emergency hatch. Kneel astern of hatch and remain plugged in on intercom. In this drill the navigator had to go first. Minutes ticked by. Then he said,

"Whatever it was seems to be clearing itself – I'm going back to *Pan*".

I replaced the hatch, went back to my place and started again to get a fix. It must have been some ten minutes later when my eye fell on something that caused the hair on the back of my neck to stand on end. It was my parachute, still in its bucket... We didn't normally wear our chutes in the air because they hampered movement, and just wore the harness ready to clip the chute on if required. All those minutes kneeling by the hatch, ready to bale out, I'd forgotten an essential part of the drill – *to clip on my parachute!* It was some days later before I could bring myself to tell my room-mate, also a navigator, the awfulness of my blunder. He thought for a minute and then said, "I suppose any day now I must expect to see you running down the runway trying to take off by flapping your arms having forgotten the bloody aircraft, you stupid bugger!"   **R. Suppards**

THE BRAVE AND THE FAIR

At RAF Wittering in 1952, several squadrons of Canberra jets were operational. Crewed by one pilot and two navigators, these aircraft were fitted with cartridge operated ejection seats for all crew members. Rumour had it that if you ejected your spine would be compressed by four inches, and that such spinal injuries would have a decidedly adverse effect on your sexual ability and desire! It was assumed that these rumours had been spread to ensure that aircrew would only eject in a desperate emergency!

On a balmy summer's morning, all 120 aircrew were assembled on the tarmac in front of No.1 hangar for something called "the ejection seat experience".

A sergeant, standing in front of a large vehicle, introduced himself to the gathered crowd, and said how proud he was to be addressing so many aircrew,

Why were Flying Instructors so rude?

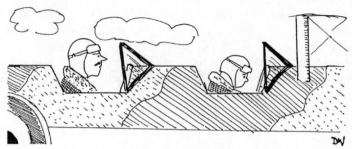

"GET YOUR GREAT SWEDE OUT OF THE OFFICE!"

"I'VE TAUGHT YOU ALL I KNOW . . . AND YOU STILL KNOW NOTHING!"

"HOW ABOUT LOWERING THE UNDERCART, CLOT!"

"IF I'D WANTED TO FLY TO HOLLAND, I WOULD HAVE TOLD YOU!"

who were without a doubt, the cream of the Royal Air Force. He was also very honoured to be given the opportunity to be involved in a training exercise, that could be of vital importance to their survival in an airborne emergency. We were willing to be impressed!

He then pressed a button on the side of his vehicle, and a meccano-like contraption reared up skywards until it almost disappeared through a thin layer of stratus. At the bottom of this contraption was – you've guessed it – an ejection seat. There was to be no escape from this training session. The sergeant once more kindly told us that we were the cream, and that our instructions were:

a) Strap yourself into the seat

b) Pull the handle

c) Experience the feel of a real ejection.

(No mention of spinal injuries etc!)

After this brief explanation he called for the first volunteer. We looked towards our intrepid squadron commander, who was never slow to demonstrate his belief in leading from the front . . . but his eyes were fixed on the hangar roof, where two pigeons were demonstrating connubial bliss.

There was not a flicker of an eyeball from all the so-called 'cream'. The sergeant displayed mock horror at the nature of the response and pleaded with us to come forward. No one moved.

The sergeant turned away, head down, and walked to a small caravan parked at the side of the hangar, and called out in an loud stage whisper

"Come out ACW Jones and give your usual demonstration to the aircrew... They are no different from those at Marham, Binbrook, Upwood, and Bassingbourn!"

The smallest WAAF you ever did see marched up to the meccano set, strapped herself in, pulled the handle, disappeared into the clouds, was wound down by the sergeant, stood up, gave a smart salute and went back to the caravan, followed by tumultuous applause.

We had been out-psyched, and in less than an hour we had all completed our ejection seat training, without any reports of spinal injury, or indeed any reports of lessening sexual activity or desire!   *Arthur Walton*

I DON'T THINK THAT'S A DRINK!   THORNEY ISLAND SUMMER 1956

It was a superb late Saturday afternoon. The Wing Sports had just finished and there was a cocktail party for the officers and their wives in the Mess. The waiters (batmen pressed into white coats for the occasion) passed amongst the guests with trays of drinks and canapes. The Pilot Officers and Flying Officers, mainly single, were trying to be as unobtrusive as possible

When Navigation Instructors were so polite!

"THAT'S TWICE YOU'VE TAKEN US THROUGH A RESTRICTED ZONE . . .
WHAT ARE YOU . . . A RUSSIAN SPY?"

"WHAT ARE YOU LOOKING UP THERE FOR . . . INSPIRATION?"

"I DON'T CARE WHAT YOU NEED TO DO URGENTLY . . . WE'RE _NOT_ IN THE FLIGHT SIMULATOR!"

WAS IT LIKE THIS FOR YOU?

with the aim of escaping the notice of the "scrambled eggs" by hiding amongst each other. Nevertheless they were making free with the drinks, telling stories and punctuating the hum of conversation with bursts of laughter. The Flight lieutenants were "sucking-up" to the Wing Commanders, and the Squadron Leaders were "crawling" to the Group Captain who was trying to get away from them so that he could do a bit of creeping with the AVM. In fact a typical formal Mess affair. Most of the ladies had clustered together, chatting away cheerfully and drinking John Collins. One Flight Lieutenant and his wife were standing apart from the rest, they were a nice couple except that she was a horsey type and had one of those loud clear voices so many horsey women seem to develop. In the hubbub of conversation it was difficult to hear oneself speak and a waiter asked her what she would like to drink. He didn't hear her and so he asked again. Just as she replied, there was one of those queer lulls when there is a seconds complete silence. So everybody heard her say, "I'd like what the rest of the ladies are having – a long cool John Thomas!"

The waiter held onto his tray with great difficulty. Silence, nobody laughed, but everybody was looking in the same direction, even the P/Os and F/Os had stopped in mid-joke. Then the noise of chatter mounted and everybody concentrated on the person they were talking to. One look at the unfortunate Flight Lieutenant showed that he was torn between murder and suicide. There was no permanent harm done, but it was a long time before, if I was with a girl, I could suppress a giggle if she asked for a John Collins!

R. Suppards

QUALIFIED PRUNES!

"CRIPES! DO A 180 SKIP,
THAT'S BUCKINGHAM PALACE
STRAIGHT AHEAD!!"

"RED TWO TO RED LEADER, IS
THAT THE NAVY FIRING AT US?"

"NO, IT'S THE REGIMENT . . .
THEY MISS US BY MORE!"

WAS IT LIKE THIS FOR YOU?

SAVED BY THE GOONS

It was 40° below, and the cold sliced through my flying clothing as "Moose" my pilot and I climbed aboard the Dakota we were slated to fly from RCAF Churchill on the Hudson Bay, to RCAF Dorval at Montreal. Take off was scheduled for 22.00 hrs. The Met Report promised clear skies, and light and variable winds. Since the clear skies meant Astro observations would be easy, and the light winds meant that track maintenance would be easy it looked as though navigation would be a doddle. Then, at the last minute we were asked to take a passenger who turned out to be a certain Strategic Air Command Chicken Colonel Muller. He was some sort of Liaison officer renowned for his derogatory views about the RAF and the RCAF. Well, I thought, the weather report couldn't be better, so he wont be able to add to his stock of bad jokes tonight at our expense. Nevertheless his presence gave me an uneasy feeling. Soon after take-off I took a routine back-bearing on Churchill and to my surprise it indicated 10° starboard drift. I discarded it. There was no way that could be right with the Met briefing I'd been given. So I decided to check it with a back bearing with the Radio Compass on Churchill Radio. All I could hear was the sound of bacon frying. I'd heard that sort of static before, it was the flippin' *Aurora Borealis*, which, when it was on display, blanked out nearly all radio signals. Alright! The Met report gave 'clear skies', so I'd take a three star fix! I pre-computed my fix and got up in the Astro-

BUT NOT ALL PRUNES WERE AIRBORNE . . .

MET BRIEFING

MET OFFICER: "CEILING ABSOLUTE, VISIBILITY UNLIMITED. YOU'LL HAVE NO DIFFICULTY FINDING YOUR TURNING POINTS TODAY!"

WEARY NAVIGATOR: "DOESN'T HE EVER LOOK OUT OF THE WINDOW?"

WAS IT LIKE THIS FOR YOU?

dome with my sextant to shoot the selected stars. Clear skies be blowed! We were socked in under ten-tenths cloud. My pre-comps were wasted. I told Moose over the intercom to climb above the cloud and at 15,000ft. We broke through only to find the brightest display of the Aurora I ever saw. The luminous green and yellow fingers spread like flame across the whole sky. It blanked out all the stars, so I told Moose to come back to our planned altitude. I was running short of options. I'd got no Radio, no Astro, and a single drift showing a 10° starboard drift, which, if I believed it, meant that I'd got a wind affecting us of 30 knots coming from the North-East. This would put me 30 miles starboard of track in an hour, and 60 miles in 2 hours. There was high ground to Starboard. I knew that if we descended through the cloud layer that was below us I could get a drift over the ground as soon as I could see the deck – or we could still be descending when we hit a stuffed cloud. It was a case of weighing options.

At the Navigation Schools there is a motto, *Man is not lost!* with the rider *...but he may be temporarily unsure of his position!* Whilst I was grappling with myself, Colonel Muller came back to look at my chart. "OK Son?" he said kindly. "Yes, thank you Colonel," I lied, thinking, "Now bugger off, and leave me alone!" Suddenly I remembered that there was another phenomenon associated with the Aurora, namely that it caused radio signals to "skip" enormous distances, and if you could recognise the Station Ident you could use (with caution) the bearing it gave you. In order to avoid talking to the Colonel, I clapped my headset to my head and began again cranking the tuning handle of the Radio Compass from one end of the frequency spectrum to the other. I should explain that when in the UK some months before, I'd been a fervent *Goon Show* fan, they were at their height in the early fifties, and in Canada away from the Goons it had taken me several months to get over the withdrawal symptoms. Then, suddenly, through all that crackling on the Radio Compass I heard, as clear as a bell Peter Sellars' voice in the guise of Nellie Crun, *"You have NOT seen a hairy bald-headed Man!"* My heart nearly stopped beating, My God! I thought, I'm over the Atlantic, I'll be cashiered! I tore off my headset, and I know I'd gone ashen. The Colonel was looking at me very curiously, but I pulled myself together. Clearly from the frequency it was a *Canadian* station, and a few checks showed that it was a broadcast from a station in Saskatchewan, nearly a 1000 miles West of Dorval! But it confirmed a strong wind from the East. Taking my heart in my hands I gave Moose a major heading alteration, and hoped for the best... Normally, from at least 100 miles out, there were half a dozen Radio stations to navigate you comfortably into Montreal, but not tonight... only the sound of frying bacon. But at last fortune smiled on me and I managed a three star fix which put me 'spot-on' for Dorval. From 30 miles or more out from Montreal, the approaching pilot can see the city, and the airfield, and Moose brought us in smooth as silk. "A good trip!" said the Colonel as he passed my position on his way off the Dak.

I had been "biting the buttons" that night, but there was one compensation. I had accidentally tuned in to the first ever transmission of *The Goon Show* in Canada. I listened to it every Thursday from then on!

R. Suppards

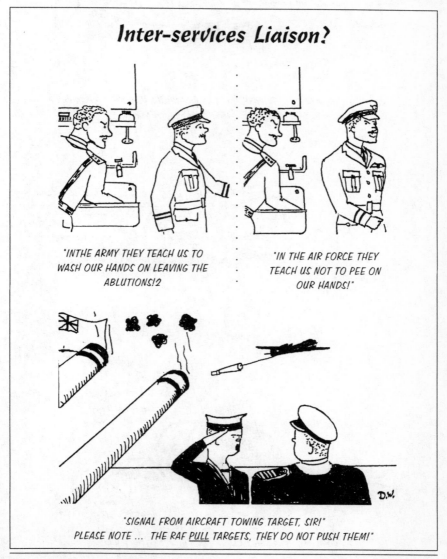

On the Flight Line

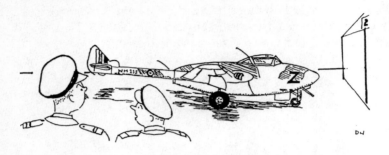

TIRED F/LT: "IN THAT CONFIGURATION IT HAS AN ENDURANCE OF 90 MINUTES."
EAGER EDUCATOR: "THEN WHAT HAPPENS?"

"LOOK UP!"
"WHAT FOR?"

"SORRY SIR . . . I CAN'T CLOSE THE CANOPY OTHERWISE!"

CHAPTER VIII

*Venture Adventure**

No commemoration of the Royal Air Force Association would be complete without mention of the Air Training Corps. It was formed in February 1941. It was formed subject to the Air Ministry and the Member of the Air Council responsible for Training Enrolment.

Candidates for enrolment were required to sign an undertaking that they were applying to join the ATC with a view to preparing themselves for wartime service with the Royal Air Force, the Naval Air Arm or the Army Air Corps. The form also made provision for the consent of the parent or guardian.

By the middle of 1942 the Air Member was able to say, "Rapid strides have been made in supplying the means for training the youth of this country with a view to providing the Royal Air Force with a wide field of selection from which to draw its future air and ground crews."

The age of Enrolment was officially 15½, but if a lad was keen, at the CO's discretion, 14-year-olds could enter.

How many of us learned Morse, Foot Drill, Engine theory, Navigation, Astro, and worked to gain our 'Star' to become a First Class cadet, and then the 'Four-bladed prop' which announced that we were 'Leading Cadets'? Certainly all those who's number started with the magic "3".

Most Squadrons paraded at least 3 times a week, with often extra 'Wings for Victory' parades, Spitfire Fund, Warship Weeks and on the VE-Day and VJ-Day parades they were given places of Honour.

The following two accounts show that both in War and Peace the Air Training Corps also had its share of people who had the potential to challenge P/O Prune when they joined the RAF.... and the third one really makes you wonder!

QUATERMASS

This story begins early one August in the fifties when I, as a cadet Flight Sergeant in the Air Training Corps, along with my squadron and three other

*The Motto of the Air Training Corps.

units of the Warwickshire and Birmingham Wing attended Summer Camp at a Royal Air Force Station somewhere in Lincolnshire.

At the time a programme called *The Quatermass Experiment* was being serialised on steam-driven black-and-white television. Such was its appeal that not one episode could be missed.

Arriving at the station mid-afternoon on Saturday, we found, to our horror, that our accommodation was to be under canvas. "How do we sweep out our bedspaces? How do you make up bed-packs on a Safari bed. Where do you stow your kit-bag?"

Having settled in it was time to explore and, as the final episode of *Quatermass* was due to be shown that evening it was imperative to find a television set so that we could all watch together.

"Right, I want twelve volunteers," I said. Such were my powers of man management that I got them (it was their first camp after all!)

"You three, find the quickest route to the NAAFI. You three, find the quickest route to the Mess Hall... You three, find out if there are any Girls Venture Corps units on this Station. And last but not least, you three, find out if there is a television we can all watch, and don't return until you've found one. Now split up and go!"

After some time, the detailed cadets returned with their success stories regarding the disposition of the NAAFI, the Mess Hall, and with the bad news that no GVC unit existed on the Station. Two of the lads on the TV search party arrived with very good news indeed.

"We've found one, Flight. You'll like it, follow us!"

Off we strode, and eventually we arrived to see, it in all its glory, an old Nissen hut! (remember those?). On entry I found it to contain, what in those days was the ultimate, a very crude TV Projection unit, multiple rows of wooden slatted chairs, and in the central aisle, not one, but two of the old 'airman's friends' – "tortoise" solid fuel stoves. Perfection indeed!

Came 18.30 hrs, and off we trooped to the Nissen Hut, the complete Flight apart from one of the TV set search party who had not been seen since being detailed off. It was with great difficulty that we found seats, as the hut was packed to the roof with cadets and airmen.

Lights out, and on with the show. Not a sound to be heard, being the final episode nobody wished to miss a thing. The serial was about to reach its big climax when the door at the rear of the hut opened and a figure made its way down the centre aisle. So gripping was the show that no one noticed the figure enter or progress down the aisle until there was an almighty "CRASH!" which caused the whole hutfull to leap off their seats in shock.

As the uproar subsided and the lights were switched on, there, sitting amongst the wreckage of a "Tortoise" stove, complete with a section of chimney piping, and about a ton of soot sat the cadet who had not returned from his quest.

Upon being questioned, as to "what the BH did he think he was up to?", he looked up at me with the biggest pair of panda eyes I had ever seen and said, "Well, Flight, I did find the TV set didn't I?" *Mike Harrison*

I BOMBED MANCHESTER.

In the Summer of 1943, I went to Chipping Warden in Oxfordshire to my first ATC camp. It was a Wimpey OTU and I was lucky enough to be listed for a four hour night Nav training flight. I was able to go to "Smokey Joes" for a night meal (two eggs – a week's ration at home!) then having drawn a parachute and been fitted with a harness I had to wait at the flight hut until I was called. There was a small problem. For those who do not remember the old high collar ATC tunic its sufficient to know that there was a First Aid pocket in the tunic where the eating irons could be stowed. They sat snugly over the left groin. With the parachute harness tight over the groin the combination was painful. Once aboard the Wimpy, the Captain seated me in the waist gun position and I had the pleasure for the first time of taking off in the dark and seeing above the cloud, the last rays of the setting sun painting the clouds rose pink and baby blue.

"NOW, REMEMBER SON . . . FLY SLOW AND FLY LOW!

The only blot on the horizon was those flippin' eating irons digging into my groin. I fidgeted them about trying to make myself more comfortable without success. They were one of my Mum's best sets of cutlery and I dare not lose them.

Then the intercom crackled, "Cadet, would you like to come up to the "office" and see how good Manchester's blackout is?"

I groped my way up the fuselage, sidling past the Navigator, and the W/Op, and suddenly in front of me where the floor should be was the square hatch that we had all come in through, open, and 10,000 feet below through thread-like wisps of cloud I could see the suburbs of Manchester sliding past. The airstream was blowing a gale upwards

into the fuselage. Could I wriggle past the hatch, or should I jump it? Taking my courage in both hands, I jumped! The rising airstream blew the skirt of my tunic up, and the last sight I had of my eating irons was as they tumbled down on Manchester.

Standing behind the pilot I could see that Manchester was ablaze with light from factories, foundries and the like, but a lot of the pleasure in this flight had evaporated. I was going to have explain to my mum how I'd lost my eating irons, but I certainly couldn't tell her that her 15 year old boy had lost them jumping over a hole in an aircraft's floor 10,000 feet up AND at 11.30 at night – long past my bedtime!   *R. Suppards*

DON'T ASSUME, UNDERSTAND!

There seems to be a common misconception that the granting of a commission in any of the services automatically endows the recipient with an enhanced level of infallibility. It also seems to be accepted that subsequent promotions automatically increase these infallibility levels. Perhaps the stories related here will serve to illustrate that links between rank and infallibility are totally mythical.

I have been associated with the Air Training Corps for a number of years, eventually rising to the rank of Flight Lieutenant and, rather rashly some may say, being entrusted with command of 1368 (Warwick) Squadron for ten years. Crimes committed during this period remained undetected and in 1980 I was asked to leave the Squadron and take a Wing Staff Officer post. I continued to cover my tracks quite well and in 1982 was promoted to the rank of Squadron Leader.

Shortly after this giant leap up the ladder of success (?) an opportunity arose to do a two week stint at RAF Bruggen in Germany as camp commandant for the ATC summer camp there. Now this was an opportunity not to be missed, a pleasant station, a good bunch of cadets, a Mini for camp running, not to mention two weeks pay at Squadron Leader rate and a duty free allowance at the end of it all. In due course various instructions arrived detailing personnel, camp programme, flight times, etc. and I duly noted that departure was to be from Luton Airport at 1100 on a Tuesday morning in July flying with Britannia Airways.

A few weeks before departure, yet another brown envelope arrived and I noted with delight that the flight was now due to be in a RAF VC-10 from Brize Norton departing at 0800. The new timing of course meant a few extra hours to settle in before launching into the camp programme and of course a far more comfortable flight (backwards) than could ever be expected in a chartered Boeing 737. Also in prospect was a good night's sleep in the terminal hotel at Brize with no early morning travelling to do. A kind neighbour had offered to drive me to Brize on the evening prior to departure so even the inconveniences of driving and car parking were eliminated.

I sat back in the secure knowledge that all was well and that my Germany trip would be a doddle... that is until the 2000 on the Sunday evening before the start of the trip. At that fateful hour I received a telephone call from the Officer who was due to escort the Cadet party to Bruggen and who had decided to make contact and exchange pleasantries before meeting me at Brize. We duly spoke for a short while and he concluded the conversation with the comment that he was looking forward to meeting me at Brize Norton the following morning since he and his party were travelling down in the early hours and not over-nighting in the hotel.

A few seconds after replacing the receiver the significance of my caller's final remark sank in. Why, if the flight was not until Tuesday morning, was he expecting to see me at Brize on Monday morning? Confidently I turned up

WHEN MRS BROWN'S LITTLE BOY COMES HOME SHE'LL FIND HE USES MORE —

CHERRY BLOSSOM
BOOT POLISH

AIR TRAING CORPS GAZETTE
MAY 1945

WAS IT LIKE THIS FOR YOU?

the movement orders, knowing that he must have made a mistake, and wondering how I could get in touch with him to explain his error. As you may by now have guessed, I had correctly noted the change of departure point and time but had totally missed the advancing of the time by 24 hours!

Now came the 'baring of the soul' time to my better half who, after a short period of complete disbelief that she could ever have married such a total prune, rallied round and undertook to complete most of my packing. I still consider it to be one of the greatest achievements in the history of mankind that I was able to check in at the Brize Norton airport hotel shortly after 2300 on that Sunday evening. The term 'White Tornado' cannot adequately describe the amount of activity in the Dawe household from 2010 onwards. A suitcase was retrieved from the loft, clothing, shoes socks etc. sorted and packed, a quick shower and a telephone call made to my boss to let him know that I would not be where he expected me to be on Monday morning. My neighbour was also alerted to the crisis and willingly (thank goodness) rose to the occasion and transported a very humble Squadron Leader to his destination.

I would like to say that this error on my part was an isolated incident, but I cannot hide the truth from friends and must admit to at least one further major instance of misreading directions since achieving an elevation in rank to Wing Commander RAFVR(T). However, that must remain another story.

John Dawe

'I COULDN'T CARE LESS THAT IT'S CHRISTMAS DAY!'

CHAPTER IX

Airmen at Play

The accounts that follow are illuminating as they show that the erk, when off duty, was not above breaking the law by such crimes as being in charge of a bike when under "the affluence of incohol", riding without lights, betting, getting drunk, getting into fights, operating a wheelchair without due care and attention and failing to be at his post when required. Also remodelling certain items of architecture. We have TWO examples of airmen positively evading the Air Force police, and inciting others to do so.

There are sidelights too on their relationships with the local talent. Much has been said of the shattering impact a "Dear John" letter could have, but perhaps there were even more which brought great relief to the recipient! How many erks on their last night of leave or on the eve of a posting, over-influenced by romantic films made promises that were given not for any deeply defined ulterior motive but simply because it seemed the right thing to do in the context of parting. These same erks now in their new location were soon kicking themselves furiously for letting their hearts rule their heads hoping for a "Dear John." If you were lucky you got one! Come to think of it we were a pretty irresponsible lot!

A FRIENDLY WORD OF ADVICE   LINCOLN, SPRING 1948

One Saturday evening both my particular oppos were away on leave and I had to be on watch at 06. 00 on Sunday morning. Rather than hang about the station on Saturday evening I decided to go to the NAAFI Club, have a meal, catch up with the newspapers, write some letters and then look in at the dance for an hour or so.

I was in the Writing Room, sitting at a desk, writing just after 21.00 hrs when suddenly the door burst open, and an American airman came sliding through it on the polished floor, on his back, feet in the air with a bleeding nose!

I stood up intending to help him to his feet but he scrambled up and took a swing at me. All in the same instant I became aware of three things:

---

1) there was a hell of a rumpus coming from the corridor outside which led from the Dance Hall – girls screaming and blokes shouting. Clearly, a fight had broken out (probably the Yanks v the rest).

2) I'd better do something about this very shirty American airman, and

3) I'd better make myself scarce before the RAFP, the MPs and the "Snowdrops" (the US Military Police) turned up. Everyone knew that when the various Service police got into high gear, complete innocence of any involvement was no guarantee of anything!

I pushed the American hard in the shoulder with the flat of my hand and said, "are the Snowdrops here yet?" He stepped back, the light of fire faded from his eyes, and he dabbed at his nose. "No", he said, his voice muffled by his handkerchief.

"Then lets get out of here," I said.

At the back of the Reading Room there was a toilet with a small window that gave onto the canal bank that ran along side of the NAAFI Club. The window hadn't been opened for a very long time, and was only about 18 inches square, but by standing on the seat, we both managed to squeeze through it and jump down onto the canal towpath. "Thanks!" he said.

Looking back we could see the Red-caps, and the Snowdrops arriving in their jeeps, and the Snowdrops were making free already with their batons.

We walked along the dark towpath for about a quarter of an hour, he told me his name was Ted and that he came from the Arkansas. Turning back we could see that airmen and soldiers were being loaded onto trucks and we waited in the shadows til the last of them had gone.

"Well," I said, "I'm going to get a bus back to camp, I've had far too much excitement for one day!"

"Yeah, " said Ted, "I guess I will too, and thanks again, for getting me out of there!"

"NO, ROMEO WON'T BE COMING OUT WITH US TODAY . . .
HE'S GOT _TWO_ BINTS WAITING FOR HIM AT THE MAIN GATE!"

WAS IT LIKE THIS FOR YOU?

"No sweat at all," I replied, "but I suggest if you get into a fight like that again you pick on somebody your own size!" (I was 6'4" and weighed over 200lbs, and he was a foot shorter and weighed no more than 125lbs). He laughed, and we went our separate ways.... **R. Suppards**

EVER BEEN HAD?

ST. EVAL 1944

I was on attachment to the Airfield Construction Unit at St Eval, and one Autumn evening I and three of my pals decided to hire bikes from the Stores and cycle down to Padstow for an evening of local generosity.

Part of our job was to get the airfield ready for operations again as quickly as possible in the event of enemy attack, crash, or whatever, and we were on stand-by from 23.59. One thing led to another and it was more like 01.59 as we started to make our unsteady way back to camp. A real pea-souper of a fog had come down whilst we were imbibing, and with no lights on our bikes we were bumping into hedges and gates/and occasionally falling off, as we made our way back to camp.

As we breasted the last hill about two miles away from St Eval we suddenly became aware that the sky over the camp was one great blaze. Crash, or enemy action – we should have been there – and we weren't. Conscience is a painful master, and being caught and punished for being absent from duty in wartime is another.

We pedalled as hard as we could, and then crept past the guardroom without booking in. But where was the fire? We should be able to find out from our fellow hut members we decided. But as we crept back into our hut we found that the rest of our crew were sound asleep. Mystified we too crept into bed.

The following morning my oppos took the bikes back to Stores and got roasted for bringing them back late. The SPs tried to give me a hard time for "forgetting" to book in the night before – but apart from that it was a normal day.

THIS LETTER SAYS THAT MY
WIFE JUST HAD A BABY . . .
BUT I'VE BEEN OVERSEAS
FOR A YEAR!"

'THAT'S NOTHING . . .
THERE'S THREE YEARS
BETWEEN ME AND MY
BROTHER!"

But where was the evidence of wrecked aircraft, bombed hangers, craters on the runway that should have been an accompaniment of that terrible fire? Why had we not been needed?

The answer came when someone said,

"Did you see FIDO last night?"

"What's that ?" I asked.

"Oh don't you know," said the other airily, "Those pipes along the runway are pumped full of petrol and then the petrol is sprayed upwards and ignited. The rising heat disperses the fog to allow the Liberators to land and take off in fog"

My qualms dispersed, and I had the odd feeling that I'd been had!

Sid Arscott

WRONG IMPRESSION!

A TYPICAL NEWSPAPER ARTICLE CIRCA 1943

"The Royal Air Force are performing herculean tasks in maintaining ever increasing pressure on Hitler's European fortress. Night and day our aircraft are sweeping the skies in their relentless pursuit of Goering's much vaunted Luftwaffe. Our airmen deserve all the praise a grateful Nation can bestow on them as they soften-up "Festung Europa" preparatory for the Day of Liberation which cannot now be long delayed.

But what the Nation must remember too is the enormous contribution made by those unsung heroes, the RAF's ground staff – the fitters and mechanics who service the aircraft. Working by day and night in the Hangers, out on the airfields, in cold, heat, rain and snow-they labour ceaselessly to get the maximum number of machines ready for battle.

What masterpieces of improvisation they perform ...

FIRST FITTER: "GOT ANY CHEWING GUM?
SECOND FITTER: "NO."
FIRST FITTER: "OH, DEAR OH DEAR! I SHALL HAVE TO USE A PROPER NUT AND BOLT!"

A YATESBURY "SMOKER"

These "smokers" often known as "Sods Operas" were put on from time to time, not only to entertain the Air Force personnel but also to entertain the local civilians. Partly I suppose to reward the nearby inhabitants for the generally tolerant way the they viewed the depredations of the local "airmanry".

It was decided apparently for this particular show to put on a couple of serious acts, as well as the "Ballet" performed by the Station rugger team, and "The Awkward Squad" performed by the WAAF and other old favourites. One was a tenor, who dressed in full evening kit sang some Italian arias. The Air Force audience sat respectfully silent for the first song. What the organizers must have been thinking of, to put this chap on, still defeats me because half the fun of going to the Station Cinema was not to watch the film, but to hear the remarks of the audience. Cries of "Give 'im the 'ook!" "Chuck 'im to the crocodiles!" or even "Get 'em orf!", would have been the likely outcome, but the pregnant silence hung like thunder in the air.

With great bravura he announced his second song. The words, "Cor Blimey", seemed to form in the air spoken from 500 lips. Then as he sang, behind him on the stage there appeared two bods with a blanket over them, and a big notice in red letters *This is a Cow*. The tenor unaware of this sang on. Moments later the 'cow' walked across the stage bearing the notice, *'As one cow said'* ... and disappeared off stage. The audience were agog! Then back came the cow crossing the stage carrying the cryptic notice *'to the other'*. The tenor was working up to his climax. Then the 'cow' reappeared for the last time bearing the notice *'Its Bull Night tonight!'*

The delighted applause, laughter, foot stamping and cheering must have made him think all his Christmases had come at once!

He bowed deeply and the curtains closed. — **R. Suppards**

NOT ON THE MAP

At this time I was a Sergeant Cartographer based at HQ Fighter Command at Bentley Priory, but my job was to ensure that all the Groups plotting tables and maps contained the latest locations of AA Sites, Observer Corps Units, Radar Stations etc. This meant that I was very often 'on attachement' somewhere or other. On this occasion I was at HQ No.9 Group based at Barton Hall in Lancashire.

At Barton Hall (which was a manor house) the Sergeants Mess was two miles away and we were issued, on temporary loan, sit-up and beg bikes to commute between the two locations. But these bikes had another use –

transport to tour the local hostelries. Six of us were feeling highly "convivial" when the time came to leave the pub we were in and make our way back to the Mess. It was dark and a fairly heated discussion arose over the choice of route back. Some favoured the route through the country lanes, but I, who's business was the intimate study of maps, favoured returning via the canal footpath which passed only a few 100 yards away from the mess. In the event opinions became sharply divided and I bet 5/- on my ability to get back first. Two other chaps came with me, the other three set off pedalling furiously on the scenic route.

For the first mile we were going like a bomb, the tow path was smooth and flat. Suddenly too late to avoid it we saw a huge hole in the tow path. I managed to avoid falling into the Canal, but my two friends went into the canal bikes and all. The blokes scrambled back up the bank looking like drowned rats – but how were we to get the bikes out? Full of alcohol-driven verve, drive and initiative, I announced that I would cycle on to the Mess Billiard Room and return with the 'rest cue', which in Lancashire they referred to as 'the groper'. I came back like a knight to the rescue, and we began 'fishing'. One bike still had its lights on, and so was easily located, the other took some 20 minutes to dredge up. Of course I lost my five bob bet, added to which I had to explain that, yes, I was a cartographer – but I could hardly be expected to know the position of every pothole in England!

Reg Sharp

RAF HOSPITAL NOCTON HALL

In the early fifties I had to have an operation on my leg. I am still too ashamed to explain why it was necessary but let us just say that it was to do with flying training. The operation was performed successfully, and I was told that I would be A1G1 again in due course. It was getting close to Christmas and it was a race against time as to whether I would heal sufficiently to be able to get home for the break.

In my ward there were eight commissioned halfwits (including myself) who were allowed to get about in wheelchairs, and Nocton Hall was a hutted hospital with small wards connected by long corridors – ideal for wheelchair racing!

After a particularly thrilling Grand Prix I crashed in the chicane and burst my stitches. The incisions started to get inflamed after re-stitching, and I required 4-hourly injections of Penicillin in opposite cheeks so to speak, and in addition collected my biggest ever roasting (and I've had a few!) from a grim-jawed, red-faced PMRAFNS battleship wearing the rank badges of a Group Captain (I was duly subdued, believe me!).

Seven Days Leave

"WELCOME HOME SON! WHEN DO YOU GO BACK?"

"NOW HERE COMES A KEEN TYPE . . . LET'S ASK HIM FOR HIS 295,
HIS 1250 AND GENERALLY GIVE HIM A HARD TIME!"

"EXCUSE PLIS . . .
COULD I THE NEXT
DANSE HAF!"

"WHY DO YOU SPEAK
TO THE GIRLS USING
AN ANGLO-POLISH
DICTIONARY?"

"BECAUSE THEY ONLY
FANCY FOREIGN
AIRMEN!"

WAS IT LIKE THIS FOR YOU?

Being less than 100% I was not taken with the rest of my ward for a Christmas visit to a cinema in Lincoln by ambulance to see a film matinee. The others in my Ward came back very much earlier than I had expected having been severally and collectively "chastened" as I had been.

In the cinema the floor had a steep slope down to the orchestra pit. A nurse sat at the end of each aisle with an occupied wheel chair at her side in the aisle. The chap nearest the orchestra pit had the brake on his chair released with the aid of a walking stick by the nit-wit behind him and went hurtling off to the orchestra pit. In turn his brake was released by the bloke behind him. In seconds there were six wheelchairs complete with occupants laughing like idiots in a heap in front of the orchestra pit. Seven nurses, seven wheelchairs complete with occupants were thrown out of the cinema. Apparently the film hadn't been much good any how!

As I remember it we all got home for Christmas I know I did- but it was more like being sent home in disgrace, than finishing a treatment!

R. Suppards

HONOUR AMONGST THIEVES   RAF DIMLINGTON, 1948

Our nearest town was Withernsea in Yorkshire. It was a little war-weary seaside town and, apart from the pubs had only two attractions: the Cinema and the Dance-hall.

The weekly Withernsea dances brought airmen from RAF Catfoss, Patrington, and Dimlington on their Saturday Liberty runs like bees to honey. Special trains used to come from Hull bringing lasses to supplement the local talent, and the New Year dance promised to be something special.

We were allowed to wear 'civvies' by this time, and we piled on to the camp's 10-tonner as happy as Larry to drive along the coast road to the dance. We had a favourite song, *Heartbreaker*, which we roared out as we drove.

The pubs did a roaring trade, the dance was great, we sang *Auld Lang Syne*, took our girls back home, or put them on the train, then went back to our truck. The other liberty trucks pulled out, and we were all assembled, except our driver! No sign of the twit! It was cold, pitch dark and getting very late.

None of us could drive and all were tight. Eventually Paddy* our cook offered to try to drive the truck back to Camp. He explained that he'd had a couple of lessons once. We agreed to give it a go and all clambered aboard and set off. Looking backwards out of the tilt we saw to our horror that he'd elected to drive along the pavement! The singing stopped. Then there was a

*Name changed to protect the guilty.

tremendous crash as Paddy tried to drive UNDER the glass canopy of the cinema! The whole erection fell into the road with an almighty shattering of glass and falling steel supports. We were very subdued by the time we got back.

In the morning the fertilizer was thoroughly in the fan! The CO interviewed each of the 30 Liberty men asking, "Who drove the truck?" He promised to stop all liberties until he found out who the culprit was. He pointed out that those with regular girlfriends would be unable to see them again until liberties were restored (there was no other way into Withernsea).

But what could we say? We were all equally guilty. I liked our CO and had severe qualms about giving the airman's stock answer, "Don't know, Sir!"

But nobody weakened and the affair remained an official mystery. I didn't see my girl for a month, and things were never quite the same with her thereafter. Fortunately I had another one at home! **_R. Suppards_**

"MY LEAVE IS UP TOMORROW . . ."

CHAPTER X

Parables and Other Stories

A PARABLE

And it came to pass, in the fullness of time, that the Hosts of the Germites and the Japites were defeated by the Democrites.

Amongst the hosts of the Democrites was the Tribe of the Raffites of Erk. The Raffites wore blue robes and drove chariots which flew, yea verily even unto the ends of the earth. And from these chariots they hurled thunderbolts at the armies of the Germites and the Japites.

But then cameth One, the Lord At-Lee, who sayeth, "Now is the Millenium, and the Raffites of Erk must beat their swords into ploughshares."

Great was the wailing and gnashing of teeth, amongst the Tribe of Raffites. Some prayed to the Great God Demob, others prayed to "Sign On" – a somewhat lesser God!

Many of the Sons and Daughters of Raff joined the Tribe of Civvy which was much concerned with making piles of shekels. Other Raffites took Chariots to Berlin, Korea, Malaya, Aden, Suez, the Falklands and even other Lands far from the sight of God.

But few of the Sons and Daughters of Raff were able to forget the days when their raiment was blue and they were eager to remember those days and to take care of Raffites less fortunate than they.

And in the 43rd year of the Nuclear Century when the Sixth George of England reigned, the Raffites built citadels where they could practice their observances.

The 310th was built in the shire of Warwick where the waters of the River Leam can be taken to improve the health of Humankind.

Still the Sons and Daughters of the Raffites labour at their self-appointed task.

A WELFARE OFFICER'S TALE

As 310 Branch Treasurer during the sixties, it became necessary for me to start deputizing for Len, our welfare officer, who sadly, was beginning to suffer from ill-health.

I had been requested from London that we paid a visit to an elderly lady who had some problems. This lady lived in the heart of the Cotswolds (such is the size of Leamington Spa, Warwick & District to officers at HQs).

Let us describe the location as: Rose Cottage, Church Lane, Little Sherbiton Under Hidicote. After one abortive mission, having navigational problems, I did on the second attempt find my target. Church Lane was a narrow, uphill, winding gravel track turning left off the Village street, the Church on my left and on each side of the track a veritable jungle of shrubbery. About half a mile onward I finally found "Rose Cottage" and Mrs B.... She was quite a dear, actually, and after the problems were dealt with I was entertained with a cup of tea and a slice of cake.

After taking my leave I had to go further up the lane until I found a 'skid pan' described as Lower Farm. Turning around with great difficulty I wended my way back towards the village.

I had got as far as the church graveyard when, without warning, an apparition dressed in black from head to toe leapt out of the bushes in front of my car. The resulting emergency stop: downhill, on gravel, was extremely spectacular (as was the return leap into the bushes by the apparition). When the figure ventured hesitantly out of the bushes I saw that it was a young man wearing a 'dog collar', who introduced himself as the curate. Needless to say his aerobatics were criticised in the time honoured way, dog collar or not!

After profusely apologising to me he asked,

"Are you a policeman?"

"No." I replied.

"But have you been to see Mrs B?"

"Yes," I replied, "but what gives you the impression that I'm a policeman?"

"Ah.... Well did she give you any of her seed cake?"

"Yes," I replied, "and it was very nice indeed!"

"Oh dear, oh dear!" said the curate, "That's what we think she poisoned her husband with!"

The following Anglo-Saxon must have seemed to be like a foreign language to the poor curate as he promptly disappeared back into the bushes.

Full of apprehension and no little bad temper I then proceeded back to the junction of the lane with the village street. I was about to take the right turn when three things happened simultaneously. A little white car came from the right at great speed, a bus came from the left and stopped opposite me and a police car pulled out to overtake the bus, saw the rapidly approaching white car, pulled back in and promptly slammed into the back of the bus.

My erk's instincts told me that there was only one appropriate course of action... and what followed was the fastest right-hand take-off from a standing start a Sunbeam Rapier has ever made. I was away before the glass had ceased falling!

I've never been near that village since, and I've certainly never eaten seed cake again!

Doug Castle

AN AIRMAN

An airman is a magic creature,
You can lock him out of your home,
But never out of your heart.

He likes to spend some money on beer,
He likes to spend some money on women,
He likes to spend some money on cigarettes,
He likes to spend the rest foolishly.

Only an airman can cram into his pocket:-
A little book
A pack of cigarettes
A comb
A bottle of beer,
A Church key,
A picture of Raquel Welch,
and what's left of last week's pay.

The Government supports him,
Towns tolerate him,
The girls love him,
and what's more so do we.

Contributed by J. Edwards

WAS IT LIKE THIS FOR YOU?

Three cheers for the man on the ground

Wherever you walk, you will hear people talk
Of men that go up in the air
Of the daredevil way, they go into the fray,
Facing death without turning a hair

They'll raise a big cheer and buy lots of beer,
For a pilot who's home on leave,
But they don't give a jigger
For a flight-mech or rigger
With nothing but props on his sleeve.

They just say "nice day" and then turn away,
With never a mention of praise,
And the poor bloody erk who does all the work
Just orders his own beer, and pays.

They've never been told of the hours in the cold
That he spends sealing the German's fate.
How he works on a kite, till all hours of night,
And then turns up next morning at eight.

He gets no rake-off for working "till take off"
Or helping the crew prepare
But when there's trouble its "Quick, at the double!"
The man on the ground must be there.

Each flying crew could tell it to you;
They know what this man is worth.
They know he's a part of the RAF's heart,
Even though he stays close to the earth.

He doesn't want glory, but please tell his story;
Spread a little of his fame around.
He's one of a few, so give him his due;
Three cheers for the man on the ground!

Eric Sykes, 1942

Frank Beasley has treasured this poem since he first came accross it in 1942 when he was a fitter.

An Airman's Song Sheet

Some of these titles have probably never appeared in print before – for the words apply to any old airman – and if he doesn't know them he will certainly know someone that does!

A Gallant Young Airman lay dying.
An Old Man told me before he died.
Aint it a pity?
Bloody Compton Basset.
Bill and I were shipwrecked.
Bless 'em All.
Bang-Away Lulu.
Bell-bottom Trousers.
Ball of Kirriemuir.
Come Inside You Silly B-
If I was the marrying kind.
I'd like to catch the WAAF.
If you want to be a Bolshevik.
Ivan Skavinsky Skaver.
In the Merry Month of May.
I've got sixpence.
I don't want to join the Air Force.
I don't care what becomes of me.
My Brother Sylvestre.
Old King Cole,
Ops in a Tiger.

Oh! Sir Jasper!
Oh! You ought to go to Wales!
Oh! You should see Queenie make water!
Pickin' all the big ones out.
She was poor but she was honest.
Shaibah Blues.
Sister Hannah Will Carry the Banner.
"Stuff Me!" said the King.
She was on the bridge at midnight!
The Firth of Forth.
The Scotsman Never Knew.
The Quartermasters Store.
There once was an Indian Maid.
The Yanks were Flying Fortresses.
The Filthiest Family in the Land.
They buried him R. Suppards.
This is my story.
We Volunteered.
When this bloody war is over!
We're a shower of Bastards.
We're off to see the Wild West Show.

Quiz

Here is something to test your memory in a different way!

A score of a 100% would be excellent-and it would show that you have still got all your buttons!

90% You're doing pretty well.

80% As they used to say at school – "You must try harder!"

70%-51% Lay off the booze – and try again later!

50% or below. We suggest that you report to your local RAF Recruiting Office on Monday as you were clearly not paying enough attention when you were in before, and you need to sign on for a further period of Service so that you can catch up!

FOR STARTERS

Q. What was the Monetary value of a "Good Conduct Stripe" during WW2?
Q. Name the first "enemy" aircraft shot down in WW2 by Fighter Command?
Q. The WAAF Officer i/c was often referred to as the ------------- ?

(Questions Set by Frank Beasley)

AN AFFAIR OF RANK

Q What was the rank of the blokes who had this many rings?

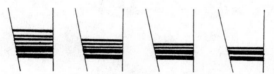

INITIAL QUIZ

What did the following initials stand for?

1.) I.T.S.	2.) I.T.W.	3.) R.T.W.	4.) S of T.T.	5.) A.G.R.S.
6.) U/S	7.) U/T	8.) E.F.T.S	9.) A.F.T.S.	10.) O.T.U.
11.) O.C.T.U.	12.) C.T.T.B.	13.) U/C	14.) A.W.O.L.	15.) A.N.S.
16.) A.O.S.	17.) C.F.S.	18.) R.T.U.	19.) A.1.G.1	20.) S.M.L.E. Mk.III
21.) L.M.G.				

MEMORY TEST

The acronym for Entertainments National Service Assn. was E.N.S.A.
The Navy Army and Air Force Institute was NAAFI.
The Auxiliary Fire Service was known as the A.F.S.
Do you remember what the Unofficial definitions were?

NICKNAMES

Some aircraft were usually better known by their nicknames than by their proper names. How many of their proper names can you remember?

1.) Annie.	2.) Lizzie.	3.) Dak.	4.) Pig.
5.) Meat-box.	6.) Wimpey	7.) Shag-bat.	8.) String-bag.
9.) Applecore.	10.) Mossie	11.) Thunderbox.	12.) Tigger.
13.) Exploder.	14.) Connie.	15.) Tiffie.	16.) Hali-bag.
17.) Hurri-bug.	18.) Widow-maker.	19.) Lib.	20.) Emily.

I.F.F. (IDENTIFICATION FRIEND OR FOE)

Next, an aircraft recognition quiz. All the types were flying in the early Months of 1945. There's some old friends and some old enemies here, can you identify them?

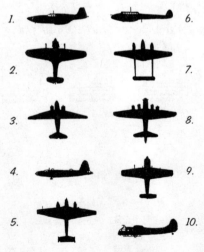

ANSWERS TO QUIZ QUESTIONS ON PAGE 123

CHAPTER XI

Demob

If you were 'In' for the Duration of Present Emergency (D of PE) your demob number was allocated on a priority system which only paid partial attention to how long you'd been 'in'.

For example, 'Boy service' was discounted, and only service after the age of 18 was counted, so if you'd volunteered you were penalized for it! It was also determined by other esoteric priorities – but once your Demob Group was confirmed as say 78 your release date was STILL in the lap of the Gods!

If you were in a Trade where replacements could be trained easily, you got out early. If you were in a Trade with a long training cycle, you got out late!

Of course, if a National Emergency was declared, as for example, the Berlin Airlift, demob was postponed indefinitely.

So you watched DROs like a hawk for two things, your Demob Group and your Trade. Sad little messages used to appear on walls such as *Roll on 78*, or *Roll on Death, Demob's a failure!*

TO AIR MINISTRY LONDON . . .
*"PLEASE ADVISE WHEN DEMOB GROUP 25 IS DUE FOR RELEASE.
SIGNED J. JONES, CORP."*

> *"All personnel proceeding on demob must clear from the outstation*
> *they are serving on and then proceed to HQ Sutton Bridge to clear,*
> *receive Demob Books, References, Rail Warrants etc. Such personnel*
> *should allow a week to complete these activities."*

Finally, that Routine Order applied to me! Along with two chaps called Ken and John, I arrived at 'The Bridge' looking to having a last easy week before reporting to 101 P.D.C. But into each life some rain must fall, and we soon realised we were going to get well doused if we didn't play our cards right. There were some thirty different places to clear from, the last being the SWO's office. In the Transit Hut we moved into, there was an unfortunate Pay Accounts Clerk who was due to go out a few days before us and who was absolutely wretched. When he'd arrived, he thought it would be a good idea to race round Sutton Bridge and get all his clearances as quickly as possible, so with three days to go before he went to Kirkham he reported to the SWO's office. The SWO promptly put him on cookhouse fatigues until it was time for him to go!

We were made of sterner stuff, and resolved that we'd done our last day's duty and, with the help of the Pay Accounts Bod we formulated a Skiving Plan to enable us to evade the SWO.

Simply put, it was: Out of the hut before 8am; NAAFI 10-11; Dinner 12.30-13.00; NAAFI 15.00-16.00; Tea at 17.00 then off Camp! In the periods where hiding was difficult, of course carrying our clearance chits we would get clearances – just about six a day, so that on Friday, the day of our departure, there would just be the SWO to clear from. We saw him about the camp from time to time, but walked past him with the air of having pressing meetings to attend.

On the Friday we got our Travel Warrants to catch the 12.30 from Sutton Bridge Railway Station, and at 10am in our best blues we reported to the SWO's Office to get his signature.

"Ah, yes," he said, "Show me your Travel Warrants."

We did as we were bid.

"Right," he said, "I've got you under my control for another two hours. I watched you three this week, and the last lesson for you to learn is that you can't beat an old skiver... Come with me!"

We followed him to the cookhouse where he showed us an absolute mountain of onions.

"Get those peeled according to the Flight Sergeant Cook's satisfaction and I'll sign your clearances!"

Never had such a mass of onions been peeled so fast!

We were red-eyed, weeping and smelling to high heaven as he gave us our chits. He smiled, showing long yellow teeth,

"If you lads are so tearful and broken up about leaving the Air Force, you can always sign-on you know!"

When we arrived at Kirkham we found three beds together and threw our kit on them. The bods on either side of us ostentatiously picked up their blankets and moved to other bedspaces as far away from us as they could get.

But then, as Ken said, "At least we did better than the Pay Accounts bod did!"

THE LAST MILE

At your final interview with the CO, he looked through your service record asked a few questions and then wrote a reference in your Airman's Release Book. The bottom line in mine was "Very Good" and "Superior". This was very kind of him, I thought, because not that long before I'd had held the Station Record for doing Jankers. Seven days for one offence, followed a week later by three days for another offence, and the day I completed that three days I copped for another three! I was innocent on all three counts, M'lud! The one I wasn't caught for was the night I crept up behind the SP who had charged me on all three occasions and heaved him into the Static Water tank! (If you re reading this Jock, I hope you caught a cold!)

In the Airman's Release book was a Railway warrant for return in case of Re-Mobilization as I looked at it, on my way by train to 101 PDC, I thought 'I won't be needing that!'

'IT'S NOT _HIS_ DEMOB . . . IT'S HIS SERGEANT'S!'

Once at Kirkham you were fed into a most efficient sausage machine of which the most memorable part was entering a hanger full of "Gent's Suitings". The choice was actually quite narrow in terms of style and materials, but there were shirts, ties, shoes socks, suits, raincoats, hats etc., and you were required to make a selection from each clothing category. I particularly remember the raincoat I chose. I needed a long one because I'm tall, but girth-wise it would have been too big round for your average elephant. All the time I had it, if I was walking into wind I had to tack, and if I was going downwind I had to run!

You handed in all your RAF kit except the uniform you were wearing. This had to be kept in case of Re-mobilization (that word again!) Your new "civvies" were packed into a cardboard box. Spivs used to hang about offering you £10 for it – but to most of us the contents of the box represented the vast majority of our civilian wardrobe and the box was not for sale.

The Air Force also gave you say, 60 days Demob leave, together with Pay warrants to draw a fortnight's pay from the post office every two weeks of your 60 days, together with appropriate Clothing Coupons and Ration Cards.

Then came a final Exit Interview with a Warrant Officer. Towards the end of his briefing he said to the group of us, "Now then lads, here is an opportunity for you to make some real money, there's a bounty if you sign-on!"

I blurted out, "I wouldn't join two pieces of string after the bloody performance I've been through in the last three years!"

He looked at me and grinned, "Do you know, its the blokes like you that are the most likely to come back in!"

I scoffed. But believe it or not, I was back in within a year – but why is another story!

•

Six of us were bound for London. Whilst the train was still in the station we drew down the blinds and started hurtling out of our uniforms and into our civvies. An elderly lady opened the carriage door and saw six young men without any trousers on! Never has a carriage door been slammed faster!

We grinned and finished changing into our dark suits, neat shirts, sober ties and green pork-pie trilby hats. We had exchanged one uniform for another! You could spot a demob suit a mile off!

The train rattled South. I looked out of the window. I was only a little over twenty years old, with three years Service, a pocket full of Clothing Coupons and Ration Cards, on my way back home. Back to my Mum and my Dad and my job at the Bank.

A few days later I saw an ad in *The Evening News*. 'Demob-type, paid on Tuesdays, broke on Thursdays, seeks similar type paid on Thursdays!'

That said it all really ... I was OUT!

THE WHEEL TURNS TWICE

The time came when the Air Force and I finally parted company and I had to re-train myself as a civilian. The years passed, we raised a family, educated them and along the way I became a reluctant gardener, decorator, plumber, toy repairer, chauffeur, paid the mortgage, took holidays every year and applied myself to my job. Almost unwittingly I became what Shakespeare called a "sober and staid citizen", grey haired and thick around the waist.

Not long ago I had to go to a meeting at Warrington near Padgate, which, due to the length of the Agenda would be a two-day effort. I was wearing a blue pinstripe suit, and driving my new car, with my briefcase on the back seat, and my suitcase in the boot. I suddenly remembered that I had not been there for nearly half a century.

For what seemed several minutes, as I drove up the main street of Warrington, I was again the 17 year old hopeful, tall, thin, wearing a jacket with the sleeves too short, shoes that let water and just ten bob in my pocket (not much different from most of my contemporaries) on my way to my first adventure in that dreadful Winter.

If I were to see him, or his ghost, what would he think of me? I don't think he would envy me – that was never his way – but he might think, "Silly old fart – I'm bound for better things!"

I delayed my meeting to drive out to Padgate, but all I could find that hadn't changed was the little Railway Station, and I thought I could see myself standing on the platform in greatcoat and full marching order bound for Pilot Grading School.

But did I envy him?

Perhaps. Everything to him was new, but not much is new to me these days, and most of what is, I don't like. Yet I know the way the Air Force moulded him, moulded me too. I'm ashamed to say that there was a lump in my throat as I turned my car round to go to my meeting.

R. Suppards

CHAPTER XII

Apocryphal Stories

Until now, all the stories in this book have been contributed by someone to whom the event happened, or to which the contributor was an eye, or earwitness. But there was another layer of stories that were told over a pint, or in the hut after lights out. If the following stories, which still lurk in the minds of ex-airmen are not true – they certainly deserve to be!

•

There is the story of the Birmingham car firm that went over to building Lancasters. One night shift there was a panic to end all panics. Somehow or other they had contrived to 'lose' 901 Lancasters! The Air Ministry "accepted" each aircraft when it came off the Production line, and somehow the records of serial numbers jumped from (say) HS2345 to HS3246! The Air Ministry called in MI5 and MI6. Everybody in the plant was under suspicion. Then the culprit came to light. There was an old chap who, armed with a set of stencils, painted the serial number on the fuselage of each Lanc as it passed his station on the production line. Somehow or other he'd made the mistake of reversing the first two digits of the serial numbers. It is said that it took two weeks for the Brummies to discover what had happened!

•

Then there is the story of the Fleet Air Arm who until 1939 painted red white and blue roundels to cover the whole chord of their aircraft wings. Admiralty ordered, after the outbreak of War, that Naval aircraft should fall in line with RAF practice which was only to cover half the chord. The reasons being that this would save paint and reduce weight. Naval Establishments applied themselves industriously to complying with the new order.

First they re-doped the whole wing, overpainting the original roundels, then they painted the new half-size roundels on the wings. This caused the consumption of dopes and paints to rocket, and made the aircraft considerably heavier!

•

A Heinkel 111 of the Luftwaffe on a dark night in the Winter of 1940. Coming back from a raid on London they'd been shot-up by AA fire, then a night-fighter had attacked them. By taking violent evasive action they had shaken the fighter off. However, the damage was such that now hopelessly lost and with the aircraft practically unflyable, there was only one decision left, to ditch! There was some argument amongst the crew as to how far across the Channel they were, but beggars cant be choosers and they pulled off a good landing in the drink. The aircraft seemed disposed to float, and they got into their dinghy without even getting their feet wet. They decided to stay by the side of their aircraft, as it would help German Air-Sea Rescue spotters find them in the morning. At Dawn's light they were chagrined to hear a Kent policeman shouting at them, "You're all under arrest!" They had ditched in the children's paddling pool at Broadstairs!

•

In the Winter of 1943, a Lancaster struggling back from the Ruhr was shot up and lost. The few winds the Navigator had been able to find were all contrary to each other denying him the possibility of finding a trend. The pilot decided to do a "wheels-up" landing whilst he still retained control of the dying aircraft. The best guess the crew could make was that the ground they could see beneath them through the breaks in the cloud was Brittany. The aircraft lobbed down, seven crew members assembled by the tail.

"Everyone OK?" asked the skipper.

"Yes, all OK," came the response.

"Right then," he continued, "we'll just set fire to A-Apple, then we must try to make contact with the French Underground to get us home!"

With A-Apple burning merrily, and ammunition exploding, the crew crouched by a hedge, and there in the light from the burning aircraft they saw a sign, 'The Kings Head', and underneath it another sign, 'You are in the Strong Country'. They were in Dorset!

•

For those who have never experienced an Arctic "white-out", let me explain. There are certain times when a snowstorm of tremendous ferocity whips up snow that has already fallen into one solid mass where sky and land merge into one white world, and in sunlight the brilliant white light is blinding. Such a phenomenon struck a USN Catalina amphibian flying over Greenland in 1943. Much of Greenland was uncharted then, but the crew felt that they were safe enough maintaining 15,000ft in the white-out conditions. Suddenly they felt a succession of gentle jolts. The ASI dropped to zero although both engines were still at three quarter throttle. Hardly daring to believe what had happened to them the pilot shut-down and the crew got out. Nervously they started to giggle. They'd flown into the top of a mountain, and on looking back they found they had been ploughing snow for nearly half a mile. They were laughing on the other side of their faces when they were eventually rescued two months later!

This story concerns a Stirling mid-upper gunner during a raid on the Ruhr. It had been an attack which had necessitated a series of long "spoof" doglegs to mislead the German night-fighters, and the Elcan (which was located directly under the mid-upper turret) was full to the brim. The lid of the Elcan was secured by a strong elastic cord.

Over the Ruhr, the Stirling was "Coned" by searchlights. The pilot, being resourceful (and strong!) dived down the beam from the lights and then hauled back on the stick hard! Inadvertently, the Stirling "looped-the loop"! At the top of the loop the elastic cord securing the lid of the Elcan gave way, and the whole of its contents fell over the gunner and his turret. Now if ever a bloke was literally in the fertilizer HE was!

•

During the closing months of the Palestine Mandate there were Spitfire squadrons flying patrols over Gaza to try to keep the peace between the emerging Israeli Air Force and the Egyptian Air Force. One RAF Pilot Officer got very bored, and spying an Arab encampment below with a large number of camels and tents, decided to buzz them. As he flew low over the encampment the camels took off in all directions. Chuckling, the pilot did a quick wing-over and came back for a second pass. Somewhere on the ground a very angry Arab picked up a clod of earth and heaved it exasperatedly at the approaching Spitfire where it lodged in the Air Cooler intake.

Rapidly the engine temperature went off the clock, and the pilot baled out. The Spitfire glided down to a landing and our hero had a long walk back to his airfield. I believe he is STILL a Pilot Officer!

•

As for being "in the fertilizer", there is the story of the ME109 pilot who baled out of his burning aircraft and crashed through the roof of a Kentish outside loo. He is alleged to have said to the Home Guard who untangled him from the ruins of the shattered bog, "I haf come out of der shit into der shit!"

•

I have often wondered if there really was a bomb-aimer who seriously said on a bombing run "Left... Left... Steady... Right... Back a bit!"

•

Another tale that has a ring of truth is the story of the Anson pilot who was given the job of flying a General from Glasgow to somewhere in the Shetlands. The General offered to navigate. The RAF half-million map showed the Shetlands in an inset on the right hand side of the chart. After some half-hour flying North the "navigator" gave the pilot an alteration of heading to 090°. Mystified, he obeyed. After some twenty minutes the pilot asked the General to show him the map. The next quandary for the pilot was this. How does a Flight Sergeant call a General a clot?

For sheer hard-headed ignorance there is this story, which takes some beating which took place in Takoradi in West Africa. During the war in the Desert aircraft were flown to Takoradi, refuelled, serviced and then flown up to join the squadrons operating in North Africa.

As the numbers of aircraft moving up this pipeline grew, the ground-crews became too thinly stretched and local African labour was taken on to do the simpler jobs. One day a Hudson came waddling in and the Flight Sergeant told one of his African helpers to inflate the tyres. Shortly afterwards the dinner bell went, and the "helper" went off for his dinner leaving the air line still attached to one of the tyres.

Another, even more un-technical African saw the grossly inflated tyre and sat down with his nose up against the wheel to see what happened next...

When the Flight Sergeant got back there was the Hudson all sad and lopsided and stretched out beside it a strange African, unconscious with an enormous lump on his head. As the tyre had burst, part of the rim of the wheel had broken off and struck him. Sensing a potential new helper, when the man recovered consciousness the Chiefy offered him a job. The African refused on the grounds that the work was too dangerous!

•

In 1943, a bumptious young Squadron Leader was a passenger in an amphibian Walrus. The flight was from Cranwell to Calshot (a flying boat base) so they took off from land but would land on water. All the way South the Squadron Leader pestered the Sergeant-Pilot to let him do the water landing, as it would be a new experience for him. Eventually, not without misgivings, the Sergeant agreed. Somewhat to the Sergeant's surprise, the Squadron Leader pulled off a very creditable landing, and the Sergeant complimented him accordingly.

The Squadron Leader waved the praise away ungraciously by saying condescendingly, "When you've got as many hours as I have, Sergeant, you'll find all aircraft are equally simple to land!"

With that, forgetting that he had landed on water, he opened the cockpit door, and stepped out into 20 feet of water!

•

Back in the golden days of the Air Force between the Wars, a great many personalities emerged in those carefree days whose light-hearted approach to the Air Force leavened the grimness of War when it came. Two such larger-than-life characters were the Atcherley twins. Ex-Cranwell cadets they were renowned for practical jokes and hairy stunts, which because of their quick wits at explaining their objectives, preserved them from the disciplinary action that almost any one else would have suffered.

In 1942 Atcherley (One), force-landed at St Eval. Learning that there was no transport available to get him to the nearest Railway Station for his return to Lincolnshire, he commandeered an ambulance and left it at the Railway Station. The Group Captain CO of St Eval fired off a snorting memo to Air Ministry where Atcherley (Two) was holding a Senior position between tours.

The reply to the furious Group Captain was on the following lines:

Dear Group Captain X,

Your letter to Air Ministry has been directed to the undersigned Wing Commander. However I am not the officer who took the ambulance. Had it been the writer, he would have taken the fire engine.

Signed.

Atcherley (Two)

.

Finally, there is the story of the satellite bomber station which sent to its Group Headquarters a teleprinter message, *'Send thirty wicker baskets'*. Three days later a party of thirty RAFPs arrived!

.

BELIEVE IT OR NOT!

I was on No.XXX Squadron on Gibraltar in 1944. Our role was the Night Air Defence of the Island. Only one fighter was used at a time, and the Duty Pilot was on 15 minutes stand-by. We used to be scrambled most nights but we were nearly always 'scrubbed' before take-off.

Fed-up with this time-wasting routine, Pete, a Pilot Officer, decided to capture one of the monkeys native to the island (known as 'rock-apes') and train it to rush out to his kite when the klaxon sounded 'scramble', switch on and then wait. Pete reckoned that if the klaxon sounded 'take-off', he'd still have plenty of time to run out to his aircraft and get airborne, otherwise he could stay in his pit, the monkey could switch off and come back to Pete's room to sleep.

One night the 'scramble' was sounded when Pete was Duty Pilot. Pete heard the Rock Ape chuntering angrily as it struggled into its little flying suit, jumped out of the hut window and ran out to the waiting aircraft. Pete heard the engine start and then dozed off... Suddenly he heard the toot of the klaxon for 'take-off'. He leapt out of bed, but too late! He heard his kite taking off!

Now that happened many years ago – but Pete is still a Pilot Officer... On the other hand, the monkey is now an Air Vice Marshal!

Answers to the Quiz

FOR STARTERS
1.) Sixpence per Day.
2.) Bristol Blenheim.
3.) The Queen Bee.

AN AFFAIR OF RANK
1.) Marshal of the Royal Air Force.
2.) Air Chief Marshal.
3.) Air Marshal
4.) Air Vice Marshal.

INITIALS
1.) Initial Training School.
2.) Initial Training Wing.
3.) Recruit Training Wing.
4.) School of Technical Training.
5.) Advanced Ground Radio School.
6.) Unserviceable.
7.) Under-training.
8.) Elementary Flying Training School.
9.) Advanced Flying Training School.
10.) Operational Training Unit.
11.) Officer Cadet Training Unit.
12.) Central Trade Test Board.
13.) Undercarriage.
14.) Absent Without Leave.
15.) Air Navigation School.
16.) Air Observers School.
17.) Central Flying School.
18.) Returned to Unit.
19.) Medical Category Fit Air and
     Ground all duties.
20.) Short Magazine Lee Enfield.
21.) Light Machine Gun (i.e. Bren)

MEMORY TEST
E.N.S.A. = Every Night Something Awful.
NAAFI. = No Ambition And no Flipping Interest.
A.F.S. = Afraid of Foreign Servicemen.

NICKNAMES
1.) Avro Anson
2.) Westland Lysander.
3.) Douglas Dakota.
4.) Vickers Valetta/Varsity.
5.) Gloster Meteor.
6.) Vickers-Armstrong Wellington.
7.) Vickers-Supermarine Walrus.
8.) Fairey Swordfish.
9.) Fairey Albacore.
10.) D.H. Mosquito.
11.) Republic Thunderbolt.
12.) D.H. Tiger Moth.
13.) Beechcraft Expeditor.
14.) Lockheed Constellation.
15.) Hawker Typhoon.
16.) Handley-Page Halifax.
17.) Hawker Hurricane.
18.) Martin Marauder.
19.) Consolidated Liberator.
20.) Kawanishi Seiku (Clear Sky)
        Naval Model 3-2.

IDENTIFICATION FRIEND OR FOE
1.) North American Mustang
2.) Hawker Hurricane
3.) Douglas Dakota.
4.) Martin Marauder
5.) ME110
6.) ME110
7.) Lockheed Lightening (P.38)
8.) Boeing Flying Fortress (B.17)
9.) Focke-Wulf 190
10.) Waco Hadrian.

PUBLISHING STANDARDS

Member Bob Stow, who starting off as a Halton apprentice finished the war as a Flight Lieutenant DFC DFM Flight Engineer with two tours on Halifaxes behind him, was complaining in the club bar about Press and Film inaccuracies on aviation matters. Several other members cited examples of Press and Film codswallop, for example, the impression given by most Battle of Britain coverage that there were no Hurricanes, Gladiators, Defiants or Blenheims involved ... only Spitfires. In the film *The Longest Day*, the Luftwaffe only had, as interceptors Me 108s (a light communications aircraft) with no gunsights, and so on.

Bob's particular gripe was with the *Daily Mirror*, which, in its wartime reports, contrived to undermine the morale of Halifax crews in a particularly depressing way. If Bomber Command attacked say Essen, the following morning the Mirror would report *Lancasters of Bomber Command attack Essen* – even if it had been an entirely Halifax show. This so cheesed off the Halifax crews that they used to refer to their aircraft as "Daily Mirror Lancasters".

WAS IT LIKE THIS FOR YOU?

More Adventures of A/c Plonk

"NO PLONK! THE PROP IS NOT SUPPOSED TO SWING YOU!"

"COULD I 'AVE A FILL FOR MY LIGHTER!"

WAS IT LIKE THIS FOR YOU?

Still More Adventures of A/c Plonk

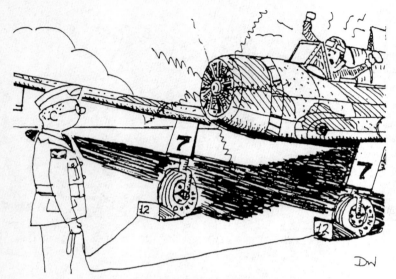

"SAY 'CHOCKS AWAY *PLEASE*'!"

"I'LL *TRY* NOT TO DROP IT SERGEANT..."

WAS IT LIKE THIS FOR YOU?

Still More Adventures of A/c Plonk

"ANY CHANCE OF ONE ON THE HOUSE FOR ONE OF BRITAIN'S FEARLESS AIRMEN?"

"THAT'S THE FIRST TIME YOU'VE EVER HIT ANYTHING PLONK ... AND IT WAS ONE OF OURS!"

"I SEE WE'VE GOT AN AC2 PLONK, P. COMING OUT ON THE NEXT DRAFT ... ANYBODY KNOW HIM?"

WAS IT LIKE THIS FOR YOU?